THE WORLD OF THE INCA

1. A characteristic view of Machu Picchu:
a street, steps and the three-windowed temple.

THE WORLD
OF THE INCA

BY

BERTRAND FLORNOY

□

TRANSLATED BY
WINIFRED BRADFORD

NEW YORK
THE VANGUARD PRESS

Library of Congress Catalogue Card Number: 56–12032

(Translated from the original French
"L'AVENTURE INCA")

Manufactured in the United States of America

To the everliving memory of
Professor Julian Tello

☐

CONTENTS

☐

ILLUSTRATIONS

□

Figs. Nos. 2–6, 16–20, 22–25, 33, 35–36, 38 and 41–43 *are reproduced from the drawings of the Peruvian Indian, Huaman Poma.*

PART ONE

□

CHAPTER I

THE COMPANIONS OF PANAMA

The village of adventure–Pizarro and his associates–Tentative explorations towards Peru–The contract of conquest

☐

'THERE were three companions at Panama, Francisco Pizarro, Diego de Almagro, and Father Ferdinand de Luque ... The leader was Francisco Pizarro, and as such, the Governor of the new province of Terra Firma appointed him captain. Almagro was a fine foot-soldier; he could follow an Indian's tracks through the thickest bush, and even if the Indian had a league's start, he could overtake him. Father de Luque was a neighbour of theirs'.

These are the opening words of the *Story of the Discovery and Conquest of Peru,* by Pedro Pizarro, cousin, page, and secretary to the leader. He introduced thus the three men who were about to reveal to sixteenth century Europe the mysterious Empire of the Sun. But in this year 1524, only a certain self-confidence distinguished our heroes amongst the troop of Spaniards stationed in the small town of Panama. A few hundred soldiers and adventurers, attracted by the golden riddle of the Indian continent, gathered round Pedrarias, the Governor of the colony. The greater number were guerrillas who had already fought in the Americas; the rest, newly arrived from Seville, knew only the marshes and jungle of the Panama Isthmus. They were all waiting for an opportunity to set out for the land washed by the Southern Sea, the Pacific Ocean, which had been discovered eleven years before by the Conquistador Balboa. They spoke of Pizarro among themselves as a captain without pity for his enemies, and without personal weakness. He had a good record of service during a campaign in a country inhabited by Caribbean cannibals, where he saw twenty of his companions killed by poisoned arrows. He was also a member of Balboa's expedition across the isthmus which divides the two oceans, and he could have described to the new arrivals from Spain the scene when Balboa took possession of the Southern Sea. For the conqueror came down to the shore, and walked into the sea in full armour, bearing on high

13

the banner of Castile. It is more likely that he maintained a discreet silence about this episode, for four years later, in 1517, he was charged with the duty of arresting Balboa, and was present at the summary execution of his old leader. Anyway Pizarro did not talk much about his exploits, and he was silent about his past.

Like the majority of the first Conquistadors, Pizarro came from Estremadura, from Trujillo. Unkind tongues had said that he was illegitimate, and that his mother sold her charms. Because of this he was abandoned on the steps of a church, and his first wet-nurse was a sow. But his father acknowledged him, and appropriately put him in charge of the pigs at his farm, later sending him to fight in Italy. They forgot to teach him to read, but that was not really necessary for a future Conquistador. No one mentioned this gossip in his presence, for his strength and his swordsmanship gave pause for reflection. In spite of his fifty years, his beard was black, and his appetites considerable. It was also rumoured that Diego de Almagro was left at a church door in Castile by his parents. Is this sad similarity in his early life the origin of his friendship for his captain, and the origin of his same courage and ignorance? In any case they had a common thirst for gold. And this passion they encountered in the third member of their company. Father de Luque, curate and then schoolmaster, was the confidant of the more prosperous members of the community. He taught grammar and the catechism to the first half-breeds of the South American continent—the eldest of his pupils was only nine. He also advised their fathers on the disposal of their wealth. One could understand his influence.

The three men met in Father de Luque's house. What was there to do in Panama but to plan new voyages? Neither extreme heat nor tropical storms could dampen their enthusiasm after listening to the accounts given by one Pascal de Andagoya, a horseman from the colony, who had undertaken several expeditions to the south, both by land and sea. During his last excursion, he was injured by a fall whilst showing off his horse in front of the Indians, but he returned with interesting tales of the southern continent. There was no doubt that a mighty nation lived there, whose ruler claimed divine origin. Indians said that gold was used widely there, and that the name of the country was Piru.

This was all that Andagoya had to tell, but Pizarro recalled that a young native who had overturned Balboa's scales, when they were filled with precious metal, excused himself by saying, 'I know a country where they eat and drink from gold vessels', and he pointed towards the south. Other information arriving at this time described animals called llamas, half camel, half sheep, and other curiosities of interest to naturalists. But the Conquistadors were not there to study botany, and Andagoya's information, which agreed with the stories of the Indians, was enough for them.

The secret meetings in the priest's house passed unnoticed. Every man had his own little El Dorado, his golden legend in his fancy, and if the priest had his, well so much the better for him. The ill-disposed could only sneer and say *'Luque loco,* Luque the fool'. Spain herself was indifferent to what was going on in Panama, the lazy capital of Golden Castile. The colony did not live up to its name, for of the fifty caravels which each year brought the gold of the New World to Seville, very few came from this land of marshes and forests. There would be no official interference in the expedition's affairs from either the Board of Trade in Andalusia which regulated the commercial and business affairs of the conquest, or from the Council for the Indies which administered and directed policy through the Governor. Luque, who was a man who could scent treasure from afar, was pleased about this indifference, especially as he was able to finance the expedition from private sources. One of his friends, a moneylender who preferred to remain anonymous for the time being, was prepared to provide part of the funds required, and the priest and the two captains provided money in equal shares to buy ships and equipment. As soon as these financial arrangements were completed, Luque was able to request an audience of the Governor and propose an expedition without its being necessary to request a single peso from government funds.

Pedrarias was strongly tempted by this proposal, and besides his official patronage would be rewarded by a percentage of the eventual harvest of gold from Piru. It would be unnecessary for him to request financial help from Charles the Fifth's financial officers, for this might be misunderstood. . . Later perhaps. Pedrarias agreed to the expedition's departure and offered an old ship, built ten years before by Balboa, which was crumbling away in the port of Panama. Luque recruited about one hundred men from amongst the adventurers who were weary of playing at being citizens of a tropical village. A voyage to mysterious Piru? Well, why not? The mosquitos and vampires were surely no more aggressive there than in Panama, and Indian arrows would not easily pierce Toledo armour.

To return to Europe would mean for many entry to some prison, and for others an unending struggle across impoverished plains against the eternal French. Long live Piru! And they emptied a flagon of Spanish wine in honour of new lands to be discovered.

A mere one hundred volunteers was but a small number for such an enterprise. But Christopher Columbus had scarcely any more for his first voyage. And the two ships would not hold more anyway, even if they were both ready at the same time, for the men had to be crowded in between the quarter deck and the forecastle. The Spanish caravels, well found and cheap to build, were so small that one could scarcely credit their ability to make long voyages. However these lightly constructed craft brought about the discovery, conquest, and geographical knowledge of the New World. With their two rectangular sails and a lateen-rigged canvas at the mizzen mast, they were easily manoeuvrable, and the magnetic compass and astrolabe they carried on board enabled them to steer their course. Pizarro was satisfied with the ships which the carpenters of Panama had repaired. Some of the sailors had already sailed towards the south with Andagoya, and they would be able to recognise the coast at the outset of the voyage.

In November everything was ready, and although it was the season of contrary winds over the Southern Sea, Pizarro was in a hurry to be gone. He bade farewell to Almagro and to Luque, who were remaining in Panama and who were already busy recruiting more men and building a new vessel. Pizarro was the real explorer and went ahead as a pioneer. Not one of the three friends had any doubts about the success of the voyage.

Exploration, whatever its objects, is an adventure in learning. Unknown lands and their mysterious inhabitants are sought for, and they are already destined to become part of our organised system of civilisation. And so, in a sense, an explorer is a man who represents a certain idea, or period, or faith. His struggles and his actions reflect his own civilisation and the evolutionary progress of customs and science in his own country. Indeed he brings them with him. Christopher Columbus, in aiming to reach the Indies by the western passage, was only putting to practical test the problem which the most enlightened geographers of the fifteenth century thought they had resolved on their maps.[1] In addition he was set on overcoming

[1] No doubt he made use of the information given to him by the pilot Alonzo Sanchez, who, in 1484, was carried by a storm as far as the Antilles.

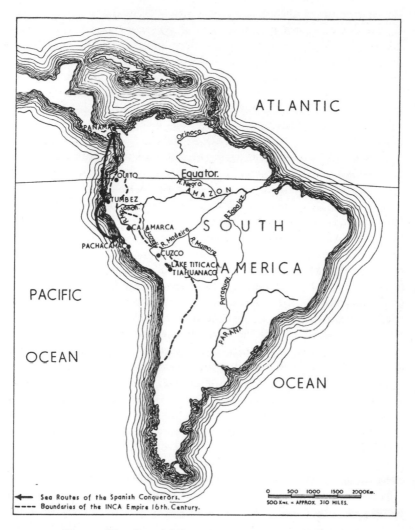

Fig. 1. The Spanish invasion of the Inca Empire

the opposition of the Spanish court, by telling them that this particular ocean route 'led to powerful countries where there were great quantities of those things they most needed : spices and precious stones'. But to force a decision, he showed the Catholic monarchs a glimpse of the glory which would be theirs if the discoveries led to the introduction of whole savage races to the Catholic religion. Columbus' arguments, together with his subsequent attitude towards the native peoples, not only reveal the character of the man, but above all bear the mark of his era.

Pizarro and his companions represent a form of conquest which Bishop Bartholomew de Las Casas was shortly to attack violently in his *Story of the Destruction of the Indies*. These explorers sought gold and nothing else. If, during their travels they came upon a truly great Empire, they would plunder it ; they had no thought at all for the native inhabitants. They would convert and baptise them and think that sufficient—that was the basic attitude of the 16th century Spaniard. But it must be remembered that the Conquistadors had to face overwhelming numbers, a hundred times superior to their own, and often hostile. They ran so many risks and met so many dangers that their indifference to the lives of others could not be wondered at. All the love and respect of which they were capable they pledged to their country and their God—a country and a God but recently freed from Moslem occupation and beliefs. Pizarro was twenty when Granada, the last Arab stronghold in Europe, surrendered to Ferdinand and Isabella, and that was the year in which Columbus discovered the New World. The adventurers passed straight from the re-conquest of their own country to the conquest of the Americas—they were still soldiers of Christ, whether fighting against the Moors or the Indians. Perhaps they even thought that the crucified God who shared their misery in the villages of Estremadura was still with them in these vast heathen territories, where fortune and glory awaited the bravest of their number. Had they not a right to a fair recompense for their gift of a new continent to their native land, of gold to their kings, and of a harvest of souls to their God ? Thus Pizarro, at the farthest point of the known world, represented a code of chivalry which was pitiless, yet convinced that its cause was just.

'On the fourteenth of November, 1525, Pizarro left the town of Panama, accompanied by one hundred and twelve Spaniards and a few Indians'.

The port of Pinas was the farthest point reached by Andagoya, and the expedition doubled this port and entered the river Biru, farther south. It may well be that the actual name of the Inca Empire originated in this native name of Biru or Piru, although the meaning of this word remains unknown to this day. Piru eventually became Peru, but for the moment it was to the Spaniards simply the territory lying beyond that river. Armed with their coats of mail or their thick doublets, Pizarro and his men disembarked and attempted their first raids into the forest. A liana slashed with a sword brushed the invaders' helmets and a breach was thus opened leading to the land of legendary gold. However the road led on into a dark forest of valleys and swamps. The men seemed for ever cut off from the sky above, and after painful marches, they threw themselves down to sleep on palm branches. The only tracks they found were those of herds of wild boar, and the only sounds they heard were the call of monkeys at dawn and the whistling of invisible birds; there were no encampments which might indicate the presence of Indians. It rained unceasingly, and the constant struggle against the mud exhausted even the strongest. Many walked barefoot. At last they reached the outskirts of the forest, but the scene offered them no encouragement, for beyond a rock-strewn plain, a bare, black mountain range enclosed the horizon. These were the Cordilleras of the Andes, and they were to be always in view as the caravels sailed down the coast. Pizarro gave the order to turn back towards the river and the sea.

They resumed their voyage, and now storm and tempest opposed the expedition's advance towards the south. For ten days the cara-vels encountered rough seas which broke open their fresh water barrels and spoiled their food. They were reduced to a miserable ration of two heads of Indian corn per day for each man. The second place of call brought no abatement of their hardships, for the virgin forest was the same, though there were fewer sounds than on the river Biru. A secretary recorded that above all, they heard the noise of the rain on the leaves. This fleeting settlement on the water's edge was named 'Port of Famine'. Food was limited to wild berries and shellfish and occasionally an animal which native servants caught in a snare, for here muskets were useless. The men began to murmur among themselves, for death had claimed twenty of their number. Pizarro rallied his party and recalled the exploits of Ojeda in the Antilles, of Ponce de Leon in Florida, and of Cortes.

But these names, which recalled victories to their captain, did nothing to ease the hunger and the fever endured by his men. Pizarro then prudently decided to send a ship to Pearl Island, near Panama, to fetch supplies.

During the two months that the caravel was away, Pizarro led his band in exploring the interior. One day they came upon a vast clearing where there was a huddle of huts. They were just in time to see the inhabitants fleeing into the undergrowth, but in the huts, which were roofed with palm branches, they found maize and fruit. The soldiers laid down their arms, and whilst they were eating like famished beasts, the Indians timidly returned to the clearing. So that was all it was! The white men were hungry, and with delightful simplicity they were ready to laugh and gather more fruit to satisfy the hungry travellers. Pizarro carefully observed the first inhabitants of these new lands, but he did not look at their faces. He could not take his eyes off the large gold ornaments they were wearing. When after two months absence the caravel returned to the Port of Famine with a cargo of flour and fresh meat, her crew found Pizarro's men ill or wounded, but clasping in their hands a few grains of gold. This ray of sunshine, gleaming in their palms, revived the Spaniards' enthusiasm. In addition to this, they learned that, after fierce battles, a powerful king, living in the mountains, had been despoiled of his kingdom by an even more powerful ruler. These new races must indeed be civilised and rich if they made war on each other! But they remained out of reach behind the stupendous wall of the Cordilleras. For the time being, Pizarro's expedition was gaining experience of the South American scene and becoming familiar with the habits of the coastal tribes. For, several leagues to the south, they came upon some families preparing a truly gruesome meal—human hands and feet simmering in a great pot over a fire. Here was a new threat to the Spaniards, and an additional reason for thinking that the lands of gold would be difficult of attainment.

Some weeks later they met armed, hostile Indians—a real indication of the danger which lay in wait for them henceforward. They had encamped near a fairly large village and had taken possession of a number of articles made of gold which they had found in the houses. Pizarro sent one of his lieutenants forward towards a mountain range, and this small band had hardly entered a pass when they were attacked by naked warriors with painted bodies, and shooting long arrows tipped with pointed bones. Three Spaniards fell dead and others were wounded. Whilst the survivors slowly withdrew, the Indians attacked Pizarro's camp. The captain himself rushed upon them with his drawn sword; he fell wounded by an arrow, but with great ferocity returned to the assault. In spite of his armour he was wounded in seven places, but with blood running freely he continued to lead the fight and beat off the attackers. At the age of fifty, he was the best of the company, and they regarded him with great respect when the battle ended. The strength and courage of their leader, even more than the jewels they had seized from their enemies, brought assurance of future victory.

However, Pizarro wisely decided to return to Panama to reinforce his men, replenish his ammunition, and to share his hopes with the Governor. There he found that Almagro himself had led a rapid campaign towards the south and had brought back gold. His losses were less severe than those of his captain, but he had been wounded by an Indian spear and had lost his right eye. But Almagro cared little about losing an eye – the one left to him had appraised the wealth of the empire which enticed the invaders by dangling gold baubles in front of them.

Father Ferdinand de Luque received his associates at his house, and they took stock of the discoveries, the financial results, and the risks of the future. But the priest no longer had two adventurers before him; Pizarro and Almagro, and especially the former, had become true Conquistadors, like Ojeda, Ponce de Leon, and Velasquez, whom the captain had held up as examples to his soldiers when they became discouraged. The two knights of the Southern Sea had drawn near to a world which they suspected would be another Mexico. Their sufferings had sealed a compact with a rich and glorious future. Luque recognised in his friends' words the passion which dominates successful men, and besides he believed in the future as firmly as they did. He soon aroused the enthusiasm of his banker, whose name was now made known. He was Gaspar de Espinosa, a licentiate and former mayor of Darien (at the other side of the Isthmus)—a man well thought of and respected from what one hears. This then was the man who supplied from his gold-filled coffers the necessary support for the conquest of Peru. He even advised that the Governor Pedrarias should be completely divested of his interest in the affair, and Almagro undertook to see to this without delay.

'Very well', said Luque, 'now let us sign a contract which will bind the three of us together for ever'.

They arranged for a public scrivener to draw up a document which the priest dictated, and on March 10, 1526, the deed of contract was presented for the signature of the interested parties. It begins thus :—'In the name of the Holy Trinity, Father, Son, and Holy Spirit, three in one true God, and in the name of the Blessed Virgin Mary, we establish the following association. . .' Four pages of small writing explained the aim and functions of an earthly trinity, of whom Luque was no doubt the Holy Spirit. The shares brought by Pizarro and Almagro consisted of the Governor's authorisation to 'conquer the lands and provinces of the realm of Peru', and it was well understood that they in person were destined to undertake the conquest. The priest furnished the necessary money, for as he said, the deed of association was for three equal shares. The amount was twenty thousand pesos in gold bars.

The division of future benefits was arranged for in every field, for each of the three associates was to receive one third of the booty of lands and people, treasures, gold, silver, pearls, emeralds, diamonds and rubies. A whole page of the contract was reserved for solemn promises made by Pizarro and Almagro to observe the agreement, and for the punishments to be administered if they broke their word. They then took the oath, making the sign of the cross above the Gospels. The contract states that the two captains could not write, and they would have signed the contract with the same sign of the cross had not Father de Luque provided two witnesses who attested the contract on behalf of the two Conquistadors.

The Empire of Peru, which so far no Spaniard had seen, and which was unknown to the scholars of the age, was thus already sold, divided out and organised. Three men in a mud-walled house in Panama decreed it thus by contract in the name of their God and of their passion for gold. Peru knew nothing of it.

CHAPTER II

INCA PROPHECIES

The Incas warned of the approach of the Spaniards–The oracle of Viracocha–Death of the eleventh king

☐

I N the vast and frozen land of the Cordilleras, ten thousand feet up, nothing seemed to move. The mountain slopes, devoid of trees and rocks, swept down from the summits into the depths of the valleys. Here could be seen eucalyptus trees gleaming with varying shades of green as the wind blew over them, and close by, the line of a road was clearly marked. A man with bare legs appeared, running with swift strides, his feet beating a regular rhythm on the flat stones that paved the road. The man's clay-coloured face remained motionless on his very upright shoulders; he had the technique of a good runner, for he was a *chaski*, 'he who carries the news' throughout the Inca Empire.

Suddenly, without slackening his pace, he shouted aloud. At his call, three men came out of a stone hut some hundreds of yards away, and as the *chaski* drew level, one of them began to run at his side. During a few rapid strides, he passed on a phrase to his companion, and then, as the other man drew ahead, he slackened his pace and stopped. He had relayed the news.

Every three miles, at the side of the roads, there was a little stone house, the *chucla*, where several couriers waited day and night to receive these oral messages and pass them on to the next stage. This was the official post of the Inca Empire.

In this extreme northern province, the post had but recently been established, for the Inca armies had not long subdued this part of the country. But the system worked well and was one of the essential parts of the machinery of Peruvian administration. The *chaskis*[1] did not have to understand the words which were communicated to them, but they had to pass them on exactly. Information about harvests, war, births, the king's orders, and the whole life of the

[1] According to the historian Cobo, a message carried by these runners took three days from Cuzco to Lima, a distance of about six hundred miles.

23

Empire was entrusted to their care. Sometimes they carried knotted cords, the *quipou*, as well as the code words which enabled officials to decipher the message on the cords. But on this occasion, one word, *Viracocha*, must have surprised the runners as they passed it along. It was the name of a dead king, a sacred spirit, a god. The word spread along the flagged road through the villages, then down

Fig. 2.
Peruvian
chaski

into ravines of dry, red earth, spiked with cactus, and then up again to the desert plateau, until by the end of the day it had reached the city of Quito.

The last stages of the relay were even speedier, for, preceded by a courier who warned the people by his shouts and cleared the way, the runner forced his pace. An officer waited for him, received the word *Viracocha*, and repeated it with astonishment. The next steps of the relay were by members of the Inca hierarchy, until it reached the king. Was he at his palace of Callo to the south of the capital, or was he at Quito itself? In any case the king received the message from the superintendent of posts, who prostrated himself before the throne of stone, set in the midst of a room covered with sheets of gold.

The name of the king was Huayna Capac, a noble prince, the eleventh of the Inca dynasty, and the direct successor of a warrior king. He himself had subdued the people of the realm of Quito, and he was feared by them. But they felt a certain respect for him, for he showered gifts on the nobles he had conquered, and showed fairness in his dealings with the peasants. The daughter of the king of Quito became his first concubine. The courtiers whispered among themselves that he took such delight in this lady that he preferred Quito to Cuzco, the true capital of his Empire.

The message which had come across the Cordilleras had now reached its destination, and the wise men, the princes of the blood, and the high officers of state waited upon the king. Huayna Capac repeated the words, and for the second time the name of Viracocha broke the silence. To him and to the high priests the message indicated that the white men who were masters of the lightning had reached the borders of their country.[1]

A century and a half before, a young prince of royal blood had been visited by a spirit whilst sleeping in a cave near Cuzco. This apparition had called itself Viracocha Inca, son of the Sun,[2] and brother of the founder of the dynasty. For the Peruvians, Viracocha was the supreme deity, the creator of the world. But the kings themselves were descended from the Sun, and the prince was not surprised either by the name or the sacred parentage of his visitor, and he addressed the spirit as his uncle. It seemed that the apparition had an important message to communicate, to the effect that a race living in a northern province of the Empire was preparing to revolt against the royal authority, and that serious complications would follow.

While scarcely awake, the young man reported this conversation to his father the king. He was unbelieving and consulted the omens, who confirmed the threat at once. In fact one tribe, the Chacas, did revolt, and were subdued only by the intervention of the young prince at the head of an army. He attributed his success to the spirit of his uncle, but the people, who preferred a living hero, gave the prince the name of Viracocha, and under this name he became the eighth Inca king.

But the priests, who had studied the words of the apparition more carefully, associated with them a series of earthquakes and gave a more complete version of the prophecy. The danger was not from the Chacas' rebellion, but from the appearance of bearded foreigners, who were masters of the lightning. King Viracocha was not alarmed by these predictions, but decided to raise a temple in

[1] This was the first of Pizarro's expeditions, which reached the fourth latitude south and then returned to Panama.
[2] The question of Viracocha the supreme god is dealt with in Part Two, Chapter III, and that of Viracocha Inca in Chapter IX.

honour of his spirit uncle, to recall the circumstances of his appearance and to induce him to protect the Incas in the future. This temple was a fine building, forty yards long and about thirty yards wide, with a single opening facing the east. Once inside, the visitor found himself in a narrow passage which he followed as far as the outer wall. Thence he passed through a second passage parallel to the first, and then through another. This labyrinth was made up of twelve corridors leading to the highest point of the temple. A stone staircase then led to a paved platform of black tiling and the domed roof was of stone. The king insisted upon this form of architecture, which greatly surprised his workmen, who were accustomed to roofs made of thatch or rushes affixed to beams. More astonishing still was the statue placed in this aerial chapel. It represented a tall man with a beard, clad in a long tunic. 'He held by a chain an animal of unknown origin, with lion's claws'.[1] It is claimed that the king himself carved the statue, for in spite of his description, the sculptors were unable to reproduce exactly the form of the apparition the king saw, or thought he saw.

And so this bearded Viracocha, holding a devil prisoner, and whom one reached only after twelve attempts to approach him, was he who had predicted the arrival of strangers on Inca soil. But today the word Viracocha invoked neither a god nor a spirit. The chiefs of the northern village used the word to convey to Huayna Capac that they had seen men coming from the sea, carrying fire, and that they had actually come into contact with them. The king at once called together the wise men and high priests.

Meanwhile life went on normally in the Empire, and it seemed as though only those near the throne and the high officers of state knew of the danger that threatened. There were indeed disturbing events which were reported from time to time, such as violent earth tremors and unusually high tides. And then one day, news came to Cuzco which aroused extreme emotions among the wise men. A condor pursued by a swarm of falcons fell wounded in the great square, and although this sacred bird, the messenger of the Sun, was tended carefully, he died. This was a bad omen, but worse was to follow. One clear night a soothsayer, accompanied by the high priest, came to the king and begged him to look at the sky. The

---

[1] Certain Conquistadors, when they saw this statue, thought that Saint Bartholomew had reached Peru before them and had converted the Indians. This opinion, and that expressed in certain accounts of these events, should be received with caution.

moon was encircled by a triple halo, one blood-red, one green, and the third like smoke. The soothsayer explained the phenomenon thus: 'The moon, your mother, tells you that Pachacamac, the creator and giver of life, threatens your family, your realm, and your subjects. Your sons will wage a cruel war, those of royal blood will die, and the Empire will disappear'. Huayna Capac called others skilled in divination, and they all interpreted the celestial portents in the same way.

The king continued to seek help from the gods. He consulted his horoscope and found there reasons for anxiety. Was he not the eleventh king? Perhaps he also thought of the temple built by his ancestor Viracocha, with its twelve corridors. And the twelfth corridor led to the round chapel where the statue of the spirit, with his chained beast, had been raised. As a final misfortune he caught cold after bathing in a thermal spring in the country, became feverish, and took to his bed. As his end approached, the king asked the priests to consult the gods as to which of his sons would be the most worthy to succeed him. Whilst the soothsayers undertook this ceremony of *Kalpa*, which necessitated offerings and sacrifices, Huayna Capac gathered many of his children round him, though not all of them, for he was reported to have about two hundred offspring. He asked them to have his body cut open after death. and to retain his heart and liver at his beloved town of Quito and then to carry his remains to Cuzco, the capital. Having thus established a just balance between his loves and tradition, he exhorted his two favourite sons, Atahualpa and Huascar, to live together in harmony. If the soothsayers did not bring the gods' reply before he died, he seemed to indicate that the northern part of the Empire should pass to Atahualpa, son of a favourite Quito concubine, and that Huascar, his legitimate heir, should reign over the rest of the country. At least that is what the near relatives of the king and the high officers of state understood to be his wishes. A third son, Cuynchi, had also certain rights to the throne, but he had few supporters at the palace, and besides he was in poor health.

After bidding his family farewell, the king called together the lords of his private council, the wise men, and the provincial chiefs, and (if the chroniclers are to be believed) addressed them in the following strange terms: 'Our father the Sun has revealed to me that after the reign of twelve Incas, his own children, there will appear in our country an unknown race of men who will subdue our Empire. They doubtless belong to the people whose messengers have appeared on our shores. Be sure of it, these foreigners will reach this country and fulfil the prophecy'.[1]

Having said these words, Huayna Capac marked on a stick the signs which would remind the officials of his words. He shut his eyes and obeyed the call of his father, the Sun. The high priest made ready the gold knife which was to be plunged into the king's breast.

[1] Garcilaso Inca de la Vega says that he learned these actual words from his uncle Cusi Hualpa, a former Captain of the Guard of the Peruvian king. The historian adds that the dying monarch counselled the Indians to serve and obey these strangers 'as men who will outshine you in everything, and who will have better laws and more powerful arms than you'. Here peeps out the political prudence of the half-breed. Cf. Part Two, Chapter I.

CHAPTER III

PIZARRO DISCOVERS PERU

Meeting with the first raft—A verse reveals the evil intentions of the conquerors—The thirteen faithful men—Landing at Tumbes—On the threshold of 'The Four Quarters of the World'

□

BARTHOLOMEW RUIZ looked at the coast to port. For some days the shore had had a welcoming look : there was clear sand and farther off the gentle swaying of tropical trees. At times smoke indicated the presence of a village. The shore was crowded with gesticulating copper-coloured men, but Ruiz did not put in to land. His duty was to explore the way south. and then to return to his chief, Francisco Pizarro, with information. The captain had established his camp near the river San Juan and had sent Almagro to Panama with a çargo of precious stones and gold. In return he was to bring back more soldiers to reinforce the expedition. Each had his task, and Ruiz, sailing south in good weather, with a light wind, thought his the most agreeable.

Suddenly a sailor shouted, 'A boat !' Ruiz mounted the forecastle and surveyed the scene. He saw a craft coming towards them, and surrounded by the rest of the crew, he watched this curious vessel. It could not be Spanish or even European. A great sail, filled by the wind, was bearing a sort of raft towards them at a good speed. But what a raft ! Under the pilot's directions, the caravel was brought to within a few cable lengths so that everyone could admire the enormous tree-trunks of which the raft was made—white and smooth, and bound together with ropes. On the stern part was a deck-house made of reeds and a large cabin thatched with grass. More than ten Indians were busy on the raft, some of whom tended the sail.

The caravel and the raft were now alongside, lifting on the same swell, and for the first time Spanish and Indian sailors were face to face on the great Southern Sea. A sailor cried, *'Hay mujeres!'* Indeed there were women on the raft, but also other temptations in the form of gold, silver, and fine woollen cloth in colours of yellow, red, and blue. The pilot boarded the Indian craft and listed her cargo, which contained silver mirrors, gold cups and vases, great quantities of materials, clothing so soft that it might have been made of feathers, and pottery decorated with animal paintings, and there were scales and weights for measuring gold. The raft was evidently equipped to do business!

Bartholomew Ruiz invited the Indians on board his ship and gave them trumpery wares. A pig was killed in honour of the occasion, and a difficult conversation ensued. However they all made themselves understood by means of signs, and it was discovered that the raft came from a port not far away. It was a large town with fine houses, and ruled by a powerful prince. 'Was there gold?' The Indians laughed and said there was as much gold as wood in their temples and palaces. The pilot did not hide his delight at this, and requisitioned the most interesting parts of the cargo and retained several of the Indians, whether they wished it or not, for they would be able to teach the sailors their language. Amongst them was a shrewd young man whom they christened Felipe on the spot. At first he was afraid of being eaten, thinking that his new masters were cannibals, but he soon realised his mistake. They all called him Felipillo, and he became the Spaniards' first Peruvian interpreter.

When the caravel returned to Pizarro, she was doubly welcome, as the little band had suffered many deprivations from hunger, crocodiles, and poisoned arrows. Some days later, Almagro arrived in his turn with reinforcements of eighty men and fresh provisions. This time the expedition against Peru would be really strong. Forward! with God's help.

But obstacles still raised themselves in the Spaniards' path. The farther they sailed south, the more hostility they encountered. The country was kinder, but the marshy forests peopled with wild beasts gave way to sunny beaches thronged with hostile tribes, and Indian arrows were more deadly than thorns or snake bites. At last one day, near a town which the captain's secretary called Tacamez, ten thousand Indians surrounded the Spaniards, who had disembarked some of their horses. Once again they were attacked by arrows and stones, and the invaders would certainly have been destroyed had not a horseman fallen from his mount. Instead of laughing or profiting by this mishap, the Indians fled, terrified by the sight of an animal which had broken in two. And so they were saved, in spite of themselves, by clumsiness or by fear. The soldiers were discontented and a noisy argument broke out, but the expedition was resumed, with the promise of eventual booty, but under duress of misery and bitter fighting. Pizarro and Almagro themselves fell out, and Almagro wanted to return to Panama to seek other men.

'What again?' exclaimed the captain. 'You for ever have the word Panama on your lips. You spend your time very agreeably running to and fro in your ship, whilst we wait to languish and die of hunger'. Their hands flew to their swords, and Ruiz had great difficulty in calming them, but at last they resumed their voyage in bad weather.

They decided to land on the Island of Gallo, where Pizarro set up camp, and Almagro sailed off to his beloved Panama to seek reinforcements once more. But he carried in the hold of his ship a secret weapon which was destined to wound his self-esteem deeply, and also to prejudice the expedition. This was a letter, which the writer, a foot-soldier called Sarabia, had slipped into a bale of cotton destined for the wife of the Governor of Golden Castile. The parcel was opened and a good deal of harm followed. The letter was in verse, but its sense was less agreeable in Almagro's ears than its rhyme. He and Pizarro were accused of being fellow-butchers; one recruited human beasts, and the other cut them up.

Prescott, in the *Conquest of Peru,* gives this doggerel verse as follows:—

> 'Look out, Senor Governor,
> For the drover while he's near,
> Since he goes home to get the sheep
> For the butcher who stays here'.

The expedition had its poets.

Almagro sought consolation from Ferdinand de Luque, while Pizarro on his island had to exist on crabs and indigestible seaweed. He occupied his time with reading the Gospels, and with reflecting that his enterprise had now lasted for two years, with the only result that a few degrees farther south had been explored, and some new shores traced on the maps. But these facts were hardly a source of pride; the essential things were those objects he had held in his hands. First some rudely fashioned discs or plates, later jewels, pendants, collars finely wrought with animal motifs, beautiful materials, and magnificent pottery, whose ornamentation indicated a way of life unknown to him. Without any doubt, these signs indicated that he had approached near to a great empire. But what would be the price of conquest and how many obstacles and trials must be overcome? Pizarro had no fear, for mystery and danger never shook his courage; his passion for conquest continued. And so it was his example more than his discipline which maintained the courage of his men through even worse tribulations. The moment had arrived for the leader to put himself, with one gesture, in the ranks of the true knights of olden times. The ships with supplies arrived from Panama under the command of a captain named Tafur. He brought a letter from the two other associates urging Pizarro to have courage—superfluous advice as far as he was concerned. His men welcomed the caravels with cries of deliverance, for they all wanted to return to Panama and they were unconvinced by their leaders' arguments. Then Pizarro traced a line on the sand with the point of his sword. 'Friends', he said, 'on our side are death, fighting, hunger, deprivations, and tempest, but the road leads to Peru and her wealth. On the other side is ease, but it is the road to Panama and poverty. Make your choice'. He himself crossed the line and took his place on the side of Peru. Only thirteen men followed him, first the pilot, Ruiz, then the knight Pedro de Candia, and eleven others whose names are known to history.

This gesture was that of a Conquistador, and indeed decided the conquest. Tafur and his ships sailed away to Panama, carrying with them the sick and weak. Pizarro and a handful of soldiers awaited new recruits, arms, and food. Their presence on this rock in the Southern Sea guaranteed the resumption of the expedition. They stayed there a further seven months in solitude, refugees on a tiny island, where they built huts to shelter them from the storms. For seven months they watched the horizon, and at last one sail appeared; a single ship and a few men was the miserable gift of the Governor of Panama, who fixed a time limit, moreover, for the continuation of the expedition. The tiny handful of men embarked, and Ruiz, on the advice of the Indians who had come from the raft, set sail for the south-east. The coast-line was low, sandy, or covered with irrigated fields; there were white houses on the upper slopes, but the Cordilleras still raised their heads to the east, the frontier of an unknown world. After sailing for twenty-five days, the ship entered the grey waters of a sound. They hove to for the night near a deserted island, though the Indians said that the city was less than a day's journey away.

2. The Companions
   of Panama:
   Father de Luque
   with Pizarro and
   Almagro.

   [Bibl. National,
   Paris]

3. The Landing at Tumbes.

[*Bibl. National,*

The old pilot and the faithful band, grouping themselves round Pizarro, gazed at the shore which lay only a few cable-lengths away, bathed in sunlight. They cried, 'Peru!', but Felipillo, the interpreter, corrected them, saying that it was the great city of Tumbes. He pointed out white houses and several tall buildings, palaces or temples, which stood in the heart of a green stretch of country. The Spaniards listened to the Indian's explanation, for they realised that their lives depended on him. Already balsa-wood rafts, loaded with armed men, surrounded the caravel, and without hesitation Pizarro invited the chiefs on board. They were clad in short, brightly coloured tunics, with a band of some material round their foreheads. They were astounded to find some of their own countrymen, and gazed with astonishment at everything they saw—white men, armour, iron tools, muskets,˙ standards. When the captain offered them wine they thought they were living in some dream. Felipillo gave an account of his adventures, and in the same way that he had dazzled the Spaniards with his description of the land of gold, he aroused cries of wonder and admiration from his compatriots as he boasted of the strength of the conquerors. More rafts arrived bearing more warriors, and Felipillo played his part, for having left Tumbes as a ship's boy, he returned as the ambassador of a great nation, the equal of his past masters. The Indian's vanity saved the expedition and precipitated the defeat of his own people.

Pizarro, who considered the day was won, made a speech—the first he made to the citizens of Peru. He said that his king was the most powerful in the world, and his God the true God, and that he had come to bring them the law of both king and God. As the interpreter translated these words, the Indian chiefs appeared unmoved and remained silent. Pizarro did not know that less than a century before, other invaders, the Incas, had made identical proposals to these people. Tumbes was at that time the farthest point of the independent royal kingdom of Chimu, and Inca ambassadors, coming down from the Cordilleras, had made the same promises. War had followed, and finally submission to the Inca armies. The Indians' sole reply to Pizarro's bold speech was to ask for a little wine—the temptation of ancient Europe. Columbus had overcome the first inhabitants of the Antilles with false pearls, mirrors, and caps, whilst Pizarro wormed his way into the good graces of the Peruvians with sour Castilian wine.

The next day, Alonzo de Molina, one of the thirteen volunteers from the island of Gallo, went ashore with a Negro, taking a pig and some poultry as presents for the chief of the city. On his return he could hardly speak for excitement and enthusiasm. He reported to his captain that he had seen little that was new—some houses, a fortress, a palace—but in that palace there was gold, gold, every-where. The accounts left by the soldiers taking part in the conquest are distressing reading for archaeologists, for there are no descriptions of clothing, pottery, architecture, tools, ornaments, or music. Rarely have invaders penetrated a new land with less curiosity, except of course for precious metals. But Molina brought joyful news, for he had seen women, splendid women fit for men who had been bound by a monastic chastity for more than a year. Women and gold; what more could one want? Pizarro grew impatient with his envoy, and the latter ended his tale by describing how the Negro had amused the Indians, and that they had scratched his skin to see if the colour would come off. The captain decided to send Pedro de Candia as a second emissary.

The knight landed, clad in full armour and carrying his musket on his shoulder. He intended to make use of his weapon to inspire respect in the crowd who welcomed him, and in response to the request of the chief of the city, the *curaca*. It was well known in the Empire that the strangers had the gift of lightning and thunder, and they wanted to see them use it. As the gun was fired there were cries of 'Viracocha!' The prophecy had come true. Pedro de Candia cast an observant eye on the low houses built of large, light-coloured bricks, on the water aqueducts, and on the fortress surrounded by three walls. He visited the convent of the virgins, laughed at the odd chignon of hair worn by some of the men, and inspected the soldiers' helmets and shields. They offered him a fermented maize drink in a golden vessel, and he told of the gold rings the chief of Tumbes wore in his ears. Felipillo explained that this man was a prince of the royal blood, a member of the Inca's family, and that because of his parentage he was allowed to bear the title of Inca. Pizarro determined to meet this man.

Pizarro kept a cool head and took counsel with the pilot, Ruiz. Orders were given that no one was to touch any objects of value without Pizarro's permission, and that the inhabitants were to be respected. And so all Pizarro's band passed through the streets of Tumbes, and the sun shining on their armour struck a thousand shafts of light. This handful of men, with heavy, clashing armour,

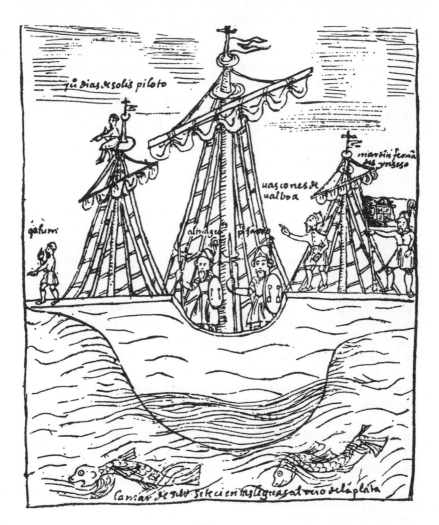

Fig. 3.
The conquerors' caravel as the Indian, Huaman Poma, saw it

hardened by years of trial, passed through the very heart of an enormous crowd, disarmed by wonder. Pizarro, at the head, bearing the banner of Castile, gazed at the Indian faces and felt that for the time being he had nothing to fear from them. The town disappointed him and he thought that Molina and Candia had been suffering from hallucinations. The houses were tiny and built of dried mud, with no doorway on the outside, and the streets were narrow and well suited for an ambush. The citizens were simply clad, without other ornament than a modest silver crescent fastened to the band across the forehead. The citadel was less imposing than Candia had described, and this would have been a considerable relief to Pizarro had he not seen paintings of fallen heads on the vessels standing at the entrance of a near-by palace. One of his companions even affirmed he saw a human head, dried and shrunken, and decorated with threads of varying colours. Pizarro passed from view into one of the patios; his interview with the Inca leader was secret, and no secretary was present. Night came and the notes of a flute and the beat of a drum were heard, in fast rhythm. The people of Tumbes were celebrating the arrival of the white men.

The Peruvian kings knew that the arrival of the strangers meant the end of their rule, but the people remembered only the prophecies and marvelled that they had come true, as the priests had foretold. They could not stop admiring these legendary beings, these sons of the Sun, these gods. Perhaps they experienced an ironical happiness in thinking of the Incas, their first conquerors, who were also sons of the Sun. After all, their grandparents had been members of an independent race; they had been Chimu before becoming an Inca dependency. They had travelled far to the north and had carried on a prosperous trade with their neighbours. Some of their customs had not been so bad after all; they buried unskilful sorcerers alive, and punished breaches of their moral code. They burned inverts in the squares, and it had amused them to see these victims dancing in the flames. Happy, happy past! Now the Inca officials raised levies for the king, or sent young men to the labour camps of the Cordillera mines.

Pressing southward on board the caravel, Pizarro's campaign along the sun-drenched shore was rather a visit of peace. As he advanced, couriers reported his coming to village after village. The balsa rafts came out from little bays and surf-fringed creeks, offering fruit, game, and fresh water to the sailors. Pizarro, relaxed and smiling, discoursed of the love of God, and his secretary records that he even refused gold objects which were offered to him. But a gold vessel with carved heads could always be bartered for a Toledo blade or for marbles! And one could not but be touched by the hospitality offered by a lady of high rank, a chief in her own right, who entertained Pizarro most pleasantly.

Under arches of flowers, amongst sweet-scented shrubs, this Peruvian lady had prepared a banquet after the fashion of her country. After the repast, the guests watched a display of music and dancing given by a band of young girls and young people in simple clothing. It was all in the best of taste and recalled the Renaissance of far-away Europe, then in its infancy. If only Ronsard could have been there!—but he was still a babe in arms, and in any case, Pizarro knew nothing of poets. Well fed and pleased by the dancing, he used this opportunity to make a speech, explaining the moral and political meaning of his presence on Peruvian soil. Then he asked his hostess to raise on high the banner of Castile, in honour of his sovereign, and this she laughingly did, saying, 'Long live Castile and Pizarro!'

After this piece of propaganda, the expedition returned to Tumbes, where Alonzo de Molina and certain others took up residence with local families. They were to await the return of their leader, who set sail for Panama with gold, silver, fine cloths, and some llamas. Pizarro was gone for longer than he had anticipated, as he went from the colony of Terra Firma to Spain, to beg Charles the Fifth to give him money and honours to mark his discovery. At the court he met the aged and embittered Cortes, who had been despoiled of his Mexican triumph in favour of a viceroy. Pizarro did not forget this lesson, and on July 26, 1529, the document which designated his powers was handed to him and he became Governor for life and Captain-General of New Castile—Peru—with a salary of seven hundred and twenty-five thousand maravedis, and almost all the prerogatives of a viceroy. He was reminded of his duty towards the native inhabitants, and especially of the law for the Indies, which enjoined him to treat these people with justice and kindness. What a victory for Francisco Pizarro! Although he had reached only part of the coastal frontier of Peru, he was already, at the Spanish court, master of the Indian Empire. His achievements and the riches he had seized from small villages assured him of greater rights than Cortes had ever had over Mexico. His destiny was now that of Spain, and the modesty of his expeditionary force, three ships, two hundred men, and twenty-seven horses, was no illusion; it was already a prince's army.

At the head of this force he left Panama on the day of St. John the Evangelist, 1531. His intention was to make direct for Tumbes, but storms drove his ships towards the shore. When he reached the first degree of north latitude, he approached an apparently easy landing place, where he disembarked his men and ordered them to advance along the coast under the protection of the three ships. The first village they came to was easily pillaged, as the inhabitants fled at the sight of soldiers with drawn swords in their hands. Pizarro employed these tactics throughout the territory to the north of Tumbes, for he knew that the natives here were still resisting the Peruvians. He risked only the hazards of battle and did not compromise the future by exacting tribute. It was thought that the people of these coastal plains were Caras, or the men who possessed emeralds. They had much gold, but precious stones also, which a Dominican friar advised them to test with hammers, and if they did not break they were genuine. In spite of this treatment, treasure worth twenty thousand pesos was gathered together. This was the first important booty taken by the Conquistadors, and Pizarro divided it out. He set aside one-fifth for the Emperor, large payments were made to the soldiers, and the rest was shared by Pizarro and his associates. This method of payment became the custom and finally the regulation during the Peruvian campaign. In this way objects of art belonging to a civilisation which thought gold was indestructible disappeared for ever, and the metal, after delivery to the skilled artisans of Europe, carried the stamp of a different world.

Farther south the Spaniards found dried corpses, which inspired them with less enthusiasm than precious metals. Miguel de Estete, who wrote his memoirs as he went along, expressed his astonishment when he entered the tombs where the people of the country, the Pasaos,[1] gathered their dead. He saw bodies from which the bones had been removed, the skin smoked and filled with straw, hung from the ceiling of the mausoleum. These were strange Indians with a proud bearing, and worshipping animals such as sharks or

[1] In the language of the Jivaro Indians, who preserve human heads, but who actually live in the Amazonian forest on the frontiers of Ecuador and Peru, the word *Pase* means that which is bad or wicked, and the word *Ao*, he or him.

peccaries which were the protectors of their tribe or trade. Miguel de Estete also discovered that these Indians preserved the heads of their dead. After removing the bones of the cranium through the neck opening, they kept the face intact with the nose, eyelids, eyebrows, and hair, and treated them in such a way that the skin and flesh were undecayed. They placed the head in so many baths of preservative that the face shrank and became smaller than that of a new-born child.[1] How fortunate were the Conquistadors to see the Jivaro technique at its best, on the shores of the Pacific! But Pizarro was no student of ethnography, and he admired, but hastened to put his own head at a safe distance.

The Governor's actions during this long march down the Peruvian coast showed that he had acquired a certain understanding of strategy in dealing with the natives, though in serious cases, the financial officer sent with him by the Council for the Indies and perhaps also some other grey-haired adviser influenced his decisions. At any rate, when he arrived with his men in the Gulf of Guayaquil, opposite Tumbes, he embarked on rafts and went, not to the Peruvian city, but to the near-by island of Puna, to await reinforcements which he expected from Nicaragua.

This island was extensive, with more than ten leagues of coast-line, well wooded, and with numerous inhabitants. These people did not speak the language of Tumbes, and dressed in a sort of loincloth, wearing their hair long or wound about their heads, or even tucked into a gourd. This amused the Spaniards, whose helmets had rather a different appearance! But these Indians were well armed, and although the chroniclers did not pay much attention to them, they did record that they had metal clubs. Felipillo warned his chief about these islanders, for they belonged to the confederation of the Caras race who lived in the valleys and mountains to the east, and were hostile to the Peruvians. Under pretext of a conspiracy by the chief of the island, a dozen or so Indians were taken prisoner and handed over to a deputation which had come from Tumbes. The slaughter which at once followed was the best present Pizarro could have given his allies. But the Caras, furious at this massacre on their own territory, blamed the Spaniards, whom they held directly responsible. There were constant attacks on Pizarro's camp, but clubs were unevenly matched against

[1] The technique of this reduction of human heads is explained in *Haute-Amazone* by the author of this book.

pikes and muskets, and for twenty days the soldiers of Castile pursued the Indians as they fled in disorder. Some chiefs were captured, and Pizarro's cousin Pedro wrote that the Governor burned some and executed others. This was good diplomacy, and after this they crossed the Gulf and disembarked peacefully at Tumbes.

Pizarro's army now numbered more than three hundred men, of whom about one hundred were horsemen, and reinforcements arrived under the command of Ferdinand de Soto.[1] Great confidence reigned in the Spanish camp, especially as Alonzo de Molina and his companions, who had been left behind at Tumbes as observers, had gathered particularly useful information about happenings in Peru. To begin with, there was no such place as Peru; the Empire was called Tawantinsuyu, which meant 'the Four Quarters of the World'. It was prey to a civil war between the two inheritors of the throne, both called Incas, and both claiming to be sons of the Sun. The Governor replied that he had heard of this from Felipillo, and asked what they had learned about the two princes. They had heard little, but they knew that Atahualpa dominated the north of the country, and Huascar, the legitimate heir, reigned in the south. Both had great ears whose lobes were widely stretched by means of rings, and these rings were of gold. Orejones—the men with the great ears—was the name given by the conquerors to the Inca kings as they prepared to invade their Empire.

---

[1] Future explorer of the Mississippi.

CHAPTER IV

HATRED AND TREACHERY

At Cuzco, the Inca Huascar assumes power–Fratricidal strife–Pizarro arrives at Cajamarca and seizes the Inca Atahualpa

□

T H E wishes of king Huayna Capac had been respected, and his heart and entrails remained at Quito, whilst his mummified body was carried to Cuzco. Well installed in his litter as if he were still alive, the Inca passed through the midst of his people as they prostrated themselves all along the road—a distance of about three hundred miles—which joined the northern province to the capital.

The procession stopped at all the houses of prayer which marked out the road, and then crossed the immense stretches of the high plateaux. In the towns, the chiefs, the priests, the heads of each community of one thousand or one hundred families, all officers of the Empire, came to weep and to praise the dead. A great number of llamas were sacrificed, and certain women who had pleased Huayna Capac during his military campaigns and who piously recalled the royal amours, begged to be allowed to join their consort in the country of the Sun. According to an Indian chronicler, they crammed into their mouths a concoction of leaves and died of suffocation. At Quito, the same fate had overtaken the wives and the most faithful servants of the king, for the great men of the Inca world never set out alone on their last journey. And so, surrounded by the grief and veneration of his people, the Inca's mummy came to Cuzco, where his son and successor, Huascar, awaited him.

The last ceremonies were ended, and the dead man, clad in his vicuña wool garments, was placed in the hall of the Sun. There he was in the company of three legitimate ancestors and five other mummies, whom the informed held to be only figureheads—the bodies of the first kings had been lost during the centuries and had been replaced by substitutes. They were all in the same attitude, with heads bent and the arms crossed on the legs, which had been folded back. They were as light as a child and were clay-coloured, and thus they defied the passage of time.

Huascar passed before his ancestors and left the temple of the Sun. Entering his litter, he returned to the palace in the centre of Cuzco, a great austere building of grey stones, shaped and inlaid. The gardens were the height of luxury, with statues of gold and silver and with inner walls adorned with gold. On reaching his chamber he called for the servants who were charged with his toilet. These were specially chosen men of high rank from the villages near by, and responsible with their lives, one for the cloaks, one for the sandals, a third for the tunics, and so on. Huascar, relieved of his ornaments, remained alone and thoughtful, the heavy gold circles in his ears the only sign of his rank.

For a whole month his duty was quite simple, as he was obliged to fast, or at least to forgo spices, as a sign of mourning. His royal tears flowed in the temple mausoleum, whilst those of his officers flowed at the same time in the town of Cuzco. He was kept informed of the official grief of the Empire and of the processions of relics. Each day the arms and insignia of the dead man were paraded amongst the people and his praises were sung. They told the glorious details of the military campaigns and the peaceful accomplishments of the departed monarch, and they sang of his justice and benevolence. Once the month was past, the ceremonies of mourning were set aside and grave considerations of government had to be faced. The king's will, giving the northern territory to Atahualpa, limited and even prevented territorial expansion, for to the east, west, and south the Empire had reached limits which it would be useless to go beyond, for neither the richness of the soil nor the skill of the inhabitants justified a further war. The north, on the contrary, was full of promise, and the realm of the Chibchas would have been an excellent acquisition. But how this region could be reached now that his brother occupied the vast intermediate state of Quito was an agonising dilemma for the king, whose first preoccupation was that of conquest. There were of course other activities, such as governing his own state, but Huascar reluctantly resolved upon a different solution. He would now have leisure to settle into their convent the virgins sent to him in homage from the provinces. His great-great-grandfather Pachacutec had produced more than three hundred offspring by his concubines, and he wanted to achieve this figure. In any case this was an easy policy to follow, and it was also his duty, for the Empire had need of a great number of sons of royal blood to fill official posts.

After five years of this monotonous task, Huascar's advisers wearied of seeing their king walking in the gardens, caressing nurselings, and amusing himself with his small sons at the circus. Trainers of wild pumas came too often to the palace. The wise men and the military leaders induced Huascar to send an embassy to Atahualpa to inform him of certain truths : that it was he, Huascar, who was the legitimate king, charged with the duty of the conquest of other countries, and that he would like his brother publicly to recognise his authority. This sudden affirmation of his rights led to the supposition that Huascar had some secret project in mind. At least that was Atahualpa's assumption when he received his brother's envoys at Quito. He sent a diplomatic reply, in which he affirmed his affection for his brother. He then without delay sent for Chalcuc-Chima and Quisquiz, his two best generals, with whom he had first campaigned when, as a young prince, he had accompanied his father on the battlefield. They decided to call together their army of veteran soldiers and to add new recruits to a total of thirty thousand men. When these preparations were sufficiently advanced, Atahualpa in his turn sent envoys to Huascar, asking him to receive himself and the representatives of the people of Quito, so that they might render solemn homage to the dead king, in the town of Cuzco, and swear an oath of fealty to their true sovereign.

So began, with the exchange of messages which were lacking in good faith, a useless fratricidal war. It was the year 1530, and the prophecies of Viracocha and of Huayna Capac were on the point of being realised. In Cuzco the king awaited the arrival of his brother. An official whose title was Tucayricuc—meaning one who sees everywhere—told the king one day that his brother had reached the gates of Tumebamba, capital of the Canaris' country, and that this was no peaceful journey, as a great army accompanied Atahualpa. The king could hardly believe the news, for his plans had not foreseen the duplicity of others. What audacity to attack the legitimate son of the Sun ! A brother who conspired against him must be slain, so Huascar could not hesitate, but ordered an army to be raised quickly in the east, west, and south of his kingdom. As a spearhead, he sent such units as were at his disposal to slow up the advance of Atahualpa's army. There were sundry clashes which were not very successful for Huascar, and some time later he was warned that bloody encounters had taken place between the people of Canaris, who were faithful to him, and his brother's troops. Atahualpa overcame Tumebamba and razed it to the ground, after which the advance speeded up and he reached the deep channel of the river Apurimac. But here the two fibre suspension bridges, the strongest in the Empire, had not even been cut. This negligence forced Huascar to group all his forces, numbering ten thousand men, on a plain three leagues from Cuzco. He could not make use of the formidable fortress of Sacsahuaman which dominated the capital on the north, for his numbers were too few, and he had to give battle on the actual invasion route.

Here were gathered soldiers of the Peruvian Empire, one against the other in spite of their common race, religion and language, for the decisive battle of a civil war. Their armaments were the same, consisting of shields, bows and arrows, javelins, clubs and slings, and the officers had short bronze swords. Over each company floated a standard which would perhaps act as a rallying point in the coming battle.

At first sunlight, a song rose from each army, seeking the protection of their god, and the companies were disclosed stretching from the heights overlooking the plain down to the strip of earth which separated them. Atahualpa's old generals stood on this day face to face with the legitimate king and his officers, all practising the same tactics of war. They would not be able to use the weapon of surprise nor the manoeuvres which for centuries they had employed against the other races of the Cordilleras. This would be a merciless struggle which the fanatics would win.

On orders from their leaders, the ranks approached within speaking distance, and according to their custom, exchanged insults. Then the archers and stone throwers went into action, as their weapons enabled them to fight at a distance, but after a time the front was broken up into isolated groups, and company fought company to the point of extermination. But Atahualpa's generals had the advantage of being able to throw in reserves to support hard-pressed units or to exploit a break-through. Huascar's soldiers, young and inexperienced, fought hand to hand, whilst those of Atahualpa, on the contrary, tried all the time to guide their enemies towards the waiting bowmen. But this form of combat required great coolness, and it was senseless and savage passions which animated the combatants on this day. The confusion was such that arrows were not retrieved, and the wounded fell and were trampled underfoot. The men from the east, whose heads were protected with animal skins, attacked relentlessly with their clubs. They struck at the legs to lower their opponents' guard, and then, with amazing speed, felled them with one blow; heads were cut open and the faces of the northerners were bathed in blood. There would have been plenty of work for the skilled Peruvian surgeons had mercy been the order of the day, but the wounded were slain and not spared. Hours passed and Huascar realised that his brother's armies

Fig. 4.
Huascar
is taken
prisoner
by his
brother's
soldiers

were being constantly reinforced and that his superior numbers now allowed him to manoeuvre his forces. They attacked the flanks, and from afar the slings were deadly. Whole companies gave ground and some fled. The eastern warriors were now thrown into the battle and it became a settling of accounts between the provinces, instead of a struggle between the two armies of the Inca princes. Eventually old-time hatreds were avenged and after several hours the fate of the battle was at last decided. The soldiers from Quito, three times superior in numbers, pursued the last Cuzco warriors, including the king, who was withdrawing in the midst of a faithful few. Quisquiz himself directed the attack so as to take Huascar alive, and just as the long red sunset streamers appeared in the sky, the king was taken prisoner, and the icy night of the Cordilleras fell on the dead and wounded.

Perhaps in the temple, where the ritual flame shone near the mummy of Huayna Capac, there was a priest who remembered the prophecies : that two sons would wage a cruel war, and royal blood would be tarnished. There was still one phrase of the oracle not yet accomplished: 'The Empire will disappear'.

During the battle, Atahualpa remained at Cajamarca, the ancient capital of a race which had submitted to the Inca rule more than a century before. The town was about two hundred leagues from Cuzco, but the news of the victory did not take as long as three days to reach the prince. The joyful tidings spread through the palace and Atahualpa was applauded as the new ruler. The next day he assumed the red turban made from vicuña wool, the insignia of the reigning Inca. He had little more to do than to keep Huascar prisoner and punish his supporters. The latter was already performed, as the northern generals had orders to punish severely the near relatives of the defeated king. In fact, a large number of his family, uncles, aunts, cousins and child nephews, was tortured and massacred. It is even said that Huascar was obliged to witness the execution of his wives and sisters. Disagreements between bastard and legitimate sons are rarely settled with courtesy.

Atahualpa, established in his new position, doubtless experienced no remorse. Huayna Capac, his father, had left the succession to the throne in such a state of uncertainty that this brutal assumption of power was almost legalised. For three generations the heir to the throne had been the most worthy son, not necessarily the eldest. No priest or soothsayer at the court could pretend that this was any other but Atahualpa. And so he gave himself up to enjoying his triumph and to preparing for his entry into Cuzco. At this moment, breathless from its long journey across the Andean valleys, strange news arrived. The white men with beards, and masters of lightning, had returned to Tumbes. They were accompanied by great four-legged beasts which could move very rapidly.

In circumstances of great difficulty, heads of states are willing to take counsel with those around them. Atahualpa continued this tradition and sought the advice of the four viceroys, his relations, who formed the grand council. They first of all decided to regroup their best troops on the plain of Cajamarca, and they debated whether to send an army to the coast. The problem was not easy,

as the inhabitants of Tumbes had always shown a certain independence, and their neighbours, the Canaris, whom Atahualpa had
recently decimated, would obviously be hostile. Besides it would be
foolish to attack without knowing the enemy's exact strength and
whether they possessed some unknown power. From this moment
the Incas had to face up to the question as to which gods would
support them in their fight against the white men. They had no
doubts about their power, for the gods had led to the borders of
the Empire men to whom the Peruvians themselves attributed the
name of Viracocha. It was well understood that men could do
nothing without the help of the gods, and the soothsayers were consulted. Finally, to complete the measures necessary for protection,
it was decided to send spies to the coastal plain to watch the invaders'
movements.

From henceforward the king was kept informed of Pizarro's
actions and movements. His occupation of Tumbes did not take
place without incident, for his soldiers, in spite of prohibitions,
pillaged the Indians who fled to the mountains, and the chief of
the town himself tried to escape. Finally everything was brought
under control, but very differently from the Inca order of things.
The groups of ten families who represented economic unity in the
Empire were broken up, and without regard for custom or family
laws, the Indians were divided out amongst new masters and
worked exclusively for them. The king was amused at this pro-
ceeding, which he considered barbarous in comparison with the
regulation of work and distribution of wealth which was put into
force in his own domains. The white men extended their influence
to the outposts of the Cordilleras and penetrated its valleys. They
advanced in small, isolated groups, so that in some villages there
were even attempts to take them by ambush, but the least signs of
any uprising were severely repressed, and thirteen chiefs were
strangled and burned at Chira. Now the invaders reached Piura, in
a fertile valley in the heart of the ancient Chimu kingdom. It was
time to act.

The Council appointed a member of the royal family to go to
the invaders' camp, disguised as a peasant, and he was to try to
learn the enemy's intentions. The Indian mingled with the Spaniards and was able to approach Pizarro. On his return he reported
that he had seen about one hundred men on foot and eighty men
mounted on what seemed to be huge sheep similar in stature to

those in the province of Collao. They wore metal clothing and carried strange arms. He considered that they were nothing more than a band of thieves—bearded, proud, and anxious. According to Pizarro's own secretary, this was the opinion that the Inca's emissary formed of the conquerors. He added that the invaders knew of the war with Huascar and of his defeat. He feared that they would seek contact with the chiefs who were faithful to the former king.

On receiving this information, Atahualpa decided that first of all Huascar's supporters must be deprived of all hope, and he ordered the guards at the fortress of Jauja, where his brother was incarcerated, to slay him without delay. He devised a plan for the total extermination of the strangers. He sent them a message with petty presents of gold and silver, giving an account of his numerous victories and his great power. But the Spanish leader replied that he himself was the subject of a royal king and that he offered, with equal loyalty, friendship or war. The Incas were puzzled by this reply and continued to watch the invaders' progress. They hesitated·as to which route to follow; some wanted to advance by the paved road leading to the south to Cuzco, but their leader chose the paths which led direct to Cajamarca. They were already at the foot of the Cordilleras, and soon they left the plain which, although arid, was intersected by many little rivers, where a number of villages served as stopping places. Their way was open as far as the steep-sided valleys.

The Inca generals were of the opinion that the time had come for a military operation, but the soothsayers had yet to give their advice, and Atahualpa decided to send an embassy to the invaders once again. They took with them as witness to their peaceful intentions ten sheep, fermented maize, and several gold cups from which to taste the drink. The message promised friendship, saying that Atahualpa would receive the strangers as brothers. Perhaps he should not have said this! For when the envoy returned to Cajamarca and reported on the interview he said that all had gone well and the bearded chief had accepted the gifts, but unfortunately an Indian in the service of the Spaniards had intervened at the end of the conversation and had grossly misbehaved. Atahualpa enquired what he had done, and the envoy said that he had pulled his ears. To pull the ears of an Inca dignitary was an insult, for in his ears he bore the rings that were the insignia of the royal family. The

4. Pre-Inca Culture: the Gate of the Sun
   at Tiahuanaco (the high plateaux).

5. Pre-Inca Culture:
   a Mochica vase (Pacific coast).

   [*Musée de l'Homme, Paris*]

reason for this gesture was that this Indian had been sent as a messenger to Cajamarca by the white leader, and had been ill-received. The envoy explained that it had not been possible for Atahualpa to receive him on account of his being in mourning, and Atahualpa commended him for giving this reply.

The strangers continued to advance. One hundred men, including forty horsemen, formed the advance guard, and their progress was cautious, as they razed each dwelling to the ground and slept in the temples. These were stone buildings erected near the roads, but always reserved for the spirits from the mountains. Sometimes chiefs were buried there and sacrifices made before sacred statues and effigies. No doubt the invaders took these buildings to be fortresses and slept there because they found that the nights grew colder as they ascended the slopes of the Cordilleras. The main body, accompanied by natives who carried their heavy, metal tubes, followed a day behind, although they joined forces when they came to a difficult passage. At last they reached a point where the mountains closed in and where an attack by the Inca army would have been child's play. But Atahualpa did not give the order to attack; he only evacuated Cajamarca of its population of two thousand inhabitants. The white men took up their quarters there, and the great Indian army encamped around the royal palace, a league from the town.

Pizarro marched out on to the plain of Cajamarca on November 15, 1532. It was eight years to the day since he had left Panama on his first expedition to Peru. And here he was, Governor and Captain-General of this Andean Empire, which by law and faith was his, at the decisive moment of entering upon his possession. In this enormous arena on a plateau at a height of ten thousand feet, surrounded by mighty summits, the scene was set for the final act of conquest. The secretary, Francisco de Jerez, noted that it was the hour of evensong, when the light from the Andes glowed upon the fields and eucalyptus trees and on great stretches of red clay on the opposite slope. Perhaps Pizarro now understood why Atahualpa had not attacked him during the long ascent, for the plain of Cajamarca was a closed battle-ground, and all its exits could be held by a few warriors. He risked annihilation. But the thought of this strategem did not halt him. Truly, in Europe a Conquistador would be but a paltry general, but here he represented the whole of

Spain, Christianity, the world, and truth. He was alone. But he had no fear; neither had he pity for his companions from Estramadura and Trujillo, his native town, should they be defeated. Solitude was strength, the crucible of his faith. He gave the order to march into Cajamarca with a group of horsemen in front, then the infantry, and finally the greater part of his cavalry. Banners were unfurled and Pizarro made a triumphal entry into a deserted city.

The central square was closed on all sides except for two gateways. The houses round the square were long, low, and solidly built, and roofed with thatch. At the side of one of the gates was a watchtower. The horses' hooves and the jangling of armour were heard in the silence, and then Pizarro said, 'Atahualpa is not here.' Ferdinand de Soto, with twenty horsemen, was sent to the Inca's camp to summon the king, and was under instructions from the Governor to proceed peacefully and to avoid a quarrel, even if the Incas appeared hostile. From the top of the tower, Pizarro gazed at the spectacle of twenty horsemen trotting through twenty thousand Indian soldiers.[1] Thinking such an embassy insufficient, he despatched his brother, Hernando, to join De Soto with fifteen more horsemen, and culverins were put into position ready to ward off danger. Whilst the Spaniards drew near to Atahualpa, the weather clouded over and a cold rain fell on the town, so Pizarro ordered his men to seek shelter, and he remained alone on the tower.

De Soto and his troop followed a wide paved road and forded two water-courses, but the Inca soldiers made no move. When they reached a parade ground the Inca king was seated on a low stone throne surrounded by four hundred officers. Two women held before him a red veil which partially hid him from sight. When the veil was drawn aside Atahualpa appeared, dignified, and wearing a turban and jewelled crown. He did not look at the Spaniards, but kept his eyes cast downward. De Soto gave him the Governor's message, and whilst it was being translated Hernando Pizarro joined the first group of horsemen.

Atahualpa did not make a direct reply, but accused the Spaniards of ill-treating the chiefs of his provinces and putting them in chains. De Soto replied that Christians offered peace to those willing to be their friends, but they made war on rebels, and in this case had

[1] Garcilaso estimated 32,000; Pedro Pizarro, 40,000; Miguel de Estete, 50,000.

exterminated them. Atahualpa then said that a chief had disobeyed him, and he invited the Spaniards to join him in a war against this man. 'Ten Christian horsemen will be sufficient to overcome him!' cried De Soto. The king smiled and ordered wine to be brought. After drinking some himself he offered some to the Spanish leaders. De Soto drank reluctantly; then, spurring his mount, he made him rear and kick, finally calming him and leading him trembling to the king's feet. Atahualpa did not flinch. Impassive, inscrutable, he allowed the horsemen to depart. His only comment was addressed to those of his subjects who had shown fear of the horses. They were executed at once.

Night fell on the myriad tents of the Inca army and on Caja-marca, where two hundred Spanish soldiers sought sleep in the damp and bare palaces of their enemies.

Next day, at dawn, the chaplain said mass and held communion; this was the Dominican, Father Vincent Valverde, whose name was to become well known later. Then envoys came to say that Ata-hualpa would visit Pizarro accompanied by armed men. Pizarro replied that armed or not, they would be awaited with friendship. Atahualpa made reply that he would come with his men unarmed and would spend one night at the Palace of the Serpent. Pizarro agreed to this, urging him to come quickly, and set about the neces-sary preparations.

This visit would be in the nature of a coronation for Pizarro and would be marked by the firing of cannon and muskets amidst cries of 'Santiago!', the name of the patron of his order of chivalry, whose shining branch was the Conquistadors. But it was to be cele-brated by battle and bloodshed, and that night, alive or dead, Pizarro would be installed as the consecrated Governor, Captain-General and supreme judge of New Castile, according to his emperor's orders. And now he allotted to all the participants their special role for this occasion. Pizarro himself would remain alone in the square, in the midst of twenty foot-soldiers, with Valverde beside him, holding the Gospels in his hand. The gunners would train their weapons on the immediate surroundings of the town, and the horsemen, divided into two companies, would wait in the neighbouring streets, whilst the foot-soldiers would hide in the houses. The trumpets would sound the alert, and each man would know what was his duty. The chaplain went from group to group saying that God was with them and would pardon their sins, whatever the outcome. It was a stupendous and terrible coronation day. Despite everything, some of the soldiers were anxious about these preparations and feared the threat which menaced them across the plain. 'They pissed with fear', the good war-correspondent Pedro Pizarro recorded.

Their fears were far from groundless, for two thousand Indians preceded the litters of the king and the provincial chief of the Caras and had already reached the outskirts of the town. A hundred dancers and singers escorted the princes, and slaves swept the paved roads where the litter-bearers would step with their bare feet. Thousands of soldiers also advanced from all sides. At the gateway of the square the escort prostrated themselves, and Atahualpa approached the terrace where Pizarro was waiting. Then in their turn, the Indians, singing, entered the square and filled the vast arena. They appeared unarmed, but an observer noted that they had slings and stones under their tunics. The city was encircled by this gigantic army.

Pizarro signed to Father Valverde to approach the king. He was followed by Hernando de Aldana, a trusted soldier, and by the interpreter Martinillo. The chaplain, on reaching the royal chair, spoke first and said that he was a priest of God and had come to tell the king what was written in the book. Atahualpa stretched out his hand, took the book and tried to open it. But it was the first time he had touched such a strange object, and the Gospels fell to the ground. Valverde picked it up whilst Atahualpa spoke of the cruelty of the Christians who had pillaged from his subjects and slain his chiefs. The priest denied this and returned to Pizarro. For a few moments everything was silent and still.

The time had come. The Governor walked slowly towards Atahualpa and gave a signal to his old friend Pedro de Candia, who commanded the artillery. A shot roared—this was the first rumbling of the storm which was about to break on the Indians. The sound of a trumpet rent the air, the clash of arms and the hammering of hooves seemed to reply, and the cry 'Santiago!' went up. The ceremony had begun. The Spaniards entered the square and threw themselves upon the Indians. Clad only in their tunics, they had no time to escape from this brutal attack. The Toledo blades carved through the masses. Blood burst from bellies that were split open and from half-severed necks. Terrified, the Indians tried to flee through the narrow gateway, and crushing each other, they fell under the musket fire. Such carnage was easy in the enclosed walls of Cajamarca. Around Atahualpa's litter, nobles, chiefs, even the head man of Cajamarca, let themselves be slain so as to protect the king with their corpses. At last a soldier reached him, and raising his sword was about to strike him down when Pizarro intervened and his own hand received the blow. He cried out that the king was his own prisoner and was not to be touched, on pain of death. The cavalry gathered outside the walls and pursued the fugitives, rushing amongst them and cutting them down without mercy. Horses and armour ran with blood; even the riders' faces were spattered with it. The ferocity of the battle, the urge to put the Empire to the sword and use the remains for their own ends, and the extravagant victory which they felt to be near, increased their strength tenfold, and besides they had never defeated so great an army. Peruvian soil would absorb the Incas' blood, but what king and what coronation had ever known such a sacrifice of human life?

At nightfall the massacre ceased and Pizarro had Atahualpa carried to a palace. In silence and with dignity the king descended and faced the Governor, who told him that he should not be offended by being a prisoner and by being defeated by the Christians, for the Spanish king was master of the whole world. The Inca people had lived in ignorance, and they would see how great were the advantages which the presence of the Spaniards would bring to their country. A captain came to make his report and to say that two thousand men had been killed, but only one Spaniard slightly wounded. There were also a few prisoners. Atahualpa still remained silent, for he could see, piled as trophies at Pizarro's feet, the familiar arms of his own people—slings and hand-polished stones as large as eggs, long clubs with pointed heads a fathom and a half long, even clubs of gold and silver belonging to his officers, and axes and spears. These arms which had triumphed over the tribes of the Cordilleras, and had even conquered his brother Huascar's armies, had been useless against a mere handful of men. He saw, however, that they laughed and drank as other men and had already seized the Indian girls, who were regarding the conquerors with languishing glances. Would he not bow his head and ask for mercy in the face of this immense, incomprehensible punishment which had befallen the Inca Empire? None of Pizarro's secretaries noticed any sign of weakness on the part of the king; on the contrary he agreed to share his conquerors' meal. Perhaps he clung to the hope that his general, Ruminaki, with the reserve army of five thousand men, would attack the next day, but Ruminaki, that same night, gathered his troops and retreated towards the north, and all was lost.

Atahualpa was treated with great consideration. He was housed in a four-storey building with an inner courtyard, where a pool was fed by hot and cold water, flowing through stone channels. His room was huge, and painted red, and here he could receive his courtiers and the officers who had escaped the massacre. Pizarro came to visit him daily and they conversed through the interpreter Felipillo, the Indian from Tumbes. The Governor learned from the king's own lips the history of his dynasty, the Inca conquests, their laws and the organisation of the labours of twelve million subjects. He learned about Cuzco, the capital, which he had not yet occupied and which remained faithful to the memory of Huascar. Atahualpa was no doubt aware that Pizarro had already established contact with his brother's old supporters and presented himself to them as the avenger of the legitimate heir, but the Inca thought he would be able to buy his freedom and spoke constantly to the Governor of the Empire's riches. Although he was a prisoner, he said that he would order his chiefs to send to Cajamarca all the precious objects in their provinces, and Pizarro could then judge for himself of the faithfulness of Atahualpa's subjects. The two men made an agreement that if Atahualpa could fill the room he occupied with gold he would be set free. At once the runners left for the provinces and brought the Inca's message to the chiefs of the larger communities. They were to bring immediately all the gold and silver objects they possessed. Before long the Indian porters marched through the Andean passes; five, ten, and finally twenty thousand pesos worth of booty arrived each day. The Spaniards calculated the wealth of the Incas in this way, since the peso was at the same time a coin and a weight. Some of the objects such as chairs and fountains with basins and statues weighed more than two hundred pounds. The secretaries had scarcely time to write down all that Indian loyalty brought in, but it weighed heavy, very heavy. Gold flowed in from everywhere, from Cuzco as well, for one of Atahualpa's brothers brought a load of jewels and gold plates and cast them at the king's feet. He was accompanied by his young sisters, and one of them was so fresh and pretty that the fifty-year-old Governor made her his queen.

Months passed. Diego de Almagro, who had not been at the

battle—he was still seeking reinforcements at Panama—arrived with about one hundred and fifty men. Pizarro had to make provision for their part and for that of the sailors, for Father de Luque, and the fifth for the king of Spain. He grew impatient and complained to Atahualpa that the gold was not arriving fast enough. The Inca indicated further sources of gold. There was Jauja, ten days march to the south, and Pachacamac, farther still on the coast, and there was Cuzco, the golden centre of the Empire. Without further delay, the Governor despatched two expeditions: one small one of three men, under the command of a brave soldier, Martin de Mogues, and a more imposing one of twenty horsemen and a few soldiers under the command of his brother Hernando. Mogues went to Cuzco and Ferdinand to Pachacamac, each preceded by a messenger from Atahualpa.

These were the first explorations made in the Cordilleras. Their aim was simple, and the accounts of their journeys reflected their one preoccupation. But Hernando Pizarro accomplished a stupendous itinerary, for he left on the eve of the Feast of Kings and returned in May, four months later, having visited Huamachuco, Pachacamac, Carhuay, Huanuco and Jauja. He traversed those parts of Peru where the traveller can still meet with monuments and legends, but his advance was blind and stubborn, a few leagues a day, travelling over passes, along rivers or deep ravines, and he took little interest in the towns he passed through, except Jauja, which he found had been built in the Spanish style. His attention was not sidetracked by fortresses nor by the wonderful suspension bridges made of plaited reeds as thick as the muscles of a man's arm. Those unaccustomed to these bridges, he said, would lose their nerve, but he did not lose a single horse in these crossings.

On arrival at Pachacamac the old passion awoke, for he found gold, and he was even impressed by the majestic temple erected on the hill overlooking the Southern Sea. He scaled five huge staircases to reach the sacred place where the idol was enthroned; he exclaimed that it was the temple of the Devil and had the old wooden idol destroyed. During four months' wanderings on the hot, empty coast, across the high plateaux swept by icy winds, and the whole length of the narrow valleys of the Cordilleras, all he sought was gold. But he met with no resistance, and in company with one of Atahualpa's faithful captains, he returned on May 8, 1533.

For twelve days the forges were alight, and the Indians, who were skilled at melting metals, transformed into ingots the treasures wrought by generations of Inca craftsmen. They produced a daily average of 50,000 pesos—four hundred and forty pounds by weight. With what Hernando Pizarro had brought, together with two hundred and twenty-five loads which Mogues added in his turn, the hearths were not yet ready to be cooled.

One cannot resist the bitter pleasure of opening at the proper page the notebook of one of the Governor's secretaries. It was not that of Pizarro's cousin Pedro, but that of Sancho de la Hoz. On June 18, 1533, the great share-out took place, and the opening account read as follows:—

	Silver Marks	Gold Pesos
To the Church	90	2,220
To the Governor Francisco Pizarro	2,350	57,220
To Hernando Pizarro	1,267	31,080
To Juan Pizarro	407	11,110
To Gonzalo Pizarro	384	9,900
To ·Juan Pizarro-Orellana	362	8,980

Besides the leader and his family, 164 horsemen and foot-soldiers, the conquerors of Cajamarca, including clerks, farriers, coopers, tailors and even one dead man, received a total of 971,125 gold pesos and 40,860 silver marks. The percentage for Almagro and his men, and for Father de Luque was all accounted for, as well as the small sums which went to the Spaniards who had remained on the Pacific coast, and especially the king of Spain's share, which far exceeded the fifth that was provided for. And it was not yet finished, for no sooner had the secretary ended his calculations than a new mass of gold arrived from Cuzco.

In this way the first conquerors of Peru were rewarded; but they knew almost nothing of this Empire of the Sun which had so suddenly enriched them. The confidences of the king, their own sufferings and struggles—that was all they knew. Before even taking possession of the country they had destroyed its laws, pillaged its wealth, and overthrown its gods without even looking at them. They were certainly brave; but encased in their armour and their own simple pride, they had already destroyed their conquest, except for Atahualpa, still prisoner in his own house at Cajamarca—and that was not to be for very long.

CHAPTER V

THE DEATH OF ATAHUALPA

The last days of the king—The execution—He who lives by the sword . . .

☐

ATAHUALPA was seated in his courtyard near the pool where hot and cold water mingled. The sky, framed by the four roofs of his prison, was the only horizon allowed to him.

No favourite was there to stretch before the king's face the purple veil which protected him from the common gaze. He was the only Inca monarch it had been possible to observe at close quarters, and truly he revealed nothing of his plight as a prisoner. Even in solitude his features remained impassive, his eyes harsh and cruel and bloodshot. Sancho de la Hoz made these observations when at times he visited the king in company with the Governor. He was tall, a little stout, and handsome; he liked to wear light, silky materials. One of his cloaks was made of the skins of birds, which he said were vampires which flew by night and attacked the people of Tumbes. When he spoke he made no gestures, his voice was harsh and his speech monotonous—he always seemed to be pronouncing judgement. He appeared to be a man of about thirty.

He called his servants. Was it not time for his meal? They spread before him a cloth of woven reeds, on which they placed cups of fermented liquor. The main dish was a stuffed lamb cut into small pieces. It was garnished with ears of maize and sweet potatoes, and of course it was highly spiced. The Indians who served the king awaited his orders, and when he pointed to a piece of meat, they offered it to him in their hands and turned away whilst he ate it. At the end of the meal they gathered up the remains and threw them into a fire—all that the Inca had touched and no longer required had to be burned. Sometimes the Governor shared his repast, and on these occasions the table was set in the main room. But these meetings were few, and Atahualpa rarely saw anyone but the members of his suite; these were the courtiers who were changed every ten days, and three of his children who shared his lot. He also

57

gave audiences to the headmen of the villages when they brought presents for his ransom. They dared not raise their eyes to the king, but sought the favour of kissing his sandals.

The Spaniards who guarded him commented on the actions of their prisoner. Thus the day that Hernando Pizarro returned from

Fig. 5.
Bringing
gifts for
Atahualpa's
ransom

his great expedition, a chief accompanied him. This was Chalcuc-Chima, the greatest of the Inca generals. Through loyalty to his prince, he had gathered together at the town of Jauja a quantity of precious metal. Before entering the presence of Atahualpa he pulled off his shoes and stockings and took with him a present for the king. On seeing his master, he flung himself on the ground, weeping and groaning, and dragged himself forward to kiss the king's hands and feet. The king accepted this homage without any show of feeling other than the formal greeting, 'You are welcome'. And Chalcuc-Chima withdrew.

The soldiers who recounted this story were conscious of the self-control and haughty demeanour of the Inca. Such a man must become a Christian. Father Valverde undertook to instruct the king in religion, and this time Atahualpa did not throw down the Gospel which the chaplain gave him. His attitude was even one of curio-sity : not only was he respectful towards the God of his conquerors, but he did not seem surprised by the doctrine of the Trinity or by other mysteries. After all was he not himself descended direct from the gods? Valverde then preached to him about humility and love of one's neighbour. Coming from the Conquistadors, the king was rather surprised by this. But he recognised that these principles were in accordance with the traditions of his own country, where the law, at least in its most inflexible aspects, applied only to the people and not to its rulers. Besides Atahualpa had a grudge against his own gods. Once he even complained about Pachacamac, who gave life to the world. 'He is a liar', said the king. Valverde was amused at this severe judgment, and asked why Pachacamac was a liar. 'When my father Huayna Capac was ill', explained the king, 'the advice of the god was sought, and he counselled a sun cure. My father died soon after. When you came to my country, I wanted to know which of us would triumph. Pachacamac said I should, but he was mistaken. Now a god cannot make mistakes—he can only lie'.

The chaplain was pleased with his pupil for a while. Had the time now come to baptise him? The ransom was almost paid; could he not be made a Christian and set free? This was the problem which beset Pizarro and his companions. With Atahualpa free, the war might spread throughout the Inca Empire. The effect of surprise no longer held good as in the early days of the conquest, for the Indians now knew the Spaniards to be men, and the whiteness of their skins was not the symbol of either peace or justice. They were three hundred against an Empire, and the most powerful weapon they possessed was Atahualpa himself. Must they abandon this weapon? De Soto, always chivalrous, then proposed that they should send the fallen sovereign to the court of Spain. If only they had listened to him the fate of the Indians would have been far different. But two men openly opposed this plan: Almagro, full of noisy talk since he had rejoined Pizarro, and the little Indian interpreter, Felipillo. This little hanger-on had become a favourite with the Conquistadors, and he would stop at nothing. For instance, he was paying court to one of the king's wives. The shabbiest rebel has always coveted royal delights. And Felipillo, since he was the link between the conquerors and the conquered, was going to play a leading part in the future of the Inca dynasty. It was he who informed Pizarro of the existence of a conspiracy. According to certain chiefs, and even some of the king's concubines, the king intended to send messengers to Quito to gather together a great army of liberation. Two hundred thousand men were said to be ready to march against Cajamarca, and amongst them thirty thousand Paltas, who were cannibals.

Pizarro reproached the king. 'I have treated you as a brother. What is this treason?'

'You are trifling with me. You jest. How can I deceive a man like you? That's enough of this joking'.

This was Atahualpa's exact reply. Francisco de Jerez heard it and noted it down the same evening. This prisoner king was not without humour. But Felipillo, on Almagro's advice, continued to collect his 'evidence'.

Pizarro was in a dilemma. He indeed esteemed the Inca highly and it was repugnant to him to kill the king in cold blood and without proof—he knew him well and the prince had loyally paid over his ransom. The two camps were in violent opposition, but at last they reached a compromise. They decided to put the king in chains. But the chain they put around his neck was not of gold as the Inca legend states; it was the heavy, final sign of the death sentence. The Governor also decided to send a mission northward to find out the truth about the army of two hundred thousand men, and De Soto undertook this assignment.

Almagro, backed by Pizarro's political adviser, protested that there had been a conspiracy and therefore there must be a trial and execution. Hernando Pizarro, the explorer's brother, who seemed to show some friendship towards the Indians, did not agree. His companion, Miguel de Estete, supported him in his opposition, the more so as he was feeling remorse for having seized Atahualpa's golden plate the day of the great massacre. To kill or not to kill? But even as the question was put, it was answered—kill. But the Governor and Captain-General of an Empire must kill legally, and so Pizarro set up a court of justice, the first European tribunal to be constituted in Peru. It was composed of a priest, Valverde, a lawyer whose name is unknown, four cavalry captains, and some assessing officers. The indictment was on three counts: treason, idolatry, and immorality. Lawyers might have objected that treason was not yet proved, that the accused was on the point of rejecting his ancient beliefs, and that marrying one's sisters was not immoral for an Inca king, since it was a traditional custom. But lawyers cannot prejudge a trial. Only the accusers were represented; the end was not justice since it was their own destiny and their own lives on which the judges must give a decision. The trial was merely the passing of a resolution, since the Inca's defenders were not present. Atahualpa did not appear. He was aware that his fate was being discussed in the room near-by and that he would not even have the right to seek the advice of the Four, who in his Empire dealt with cases of treason. But his royal justice was sufficiently speedy and cruel for him to lack any desire to make use of it. Those suspected of having acted against the safety of the state were thrown into a cave amongst ferocious wild beasts—pumas and jaguars, and also venomous snakes and serpents. The condemned man stayed there two days, and if the beasts had spared him, he regained his liberty, but such a case was rare. Atahualpa did not know the form of his punishment, but he consoled those around him by saying that if he were not condemned to the stake, the Sun would allow him one day to take his place again among men.

Pizarro came to pronounce sentence, which was that the king should be burned alive. Atahualpa remained silent at first, but then attempted to plead his cause for the last time. He said that he had paid his ransom but that other treasures remained, and that if he died, his people would no longer submit and would hide their gold and silver. Plunging his hand into a receptacle full of maize, he held up a handful, saying that he had only given up that much of his riches—the rest was hidden and would be lost.

But the Governor could only repeat the sentence of death. The king gave up hope and the invisible hand of fear passed over his face which had for so many months remained impassive; his expression altered and his eyes filled with tears. Pizarro could not hide his own emotion, for he had not the hard heart of a clerk of a tribunal. He offered the condemned man an easier death if he would be baptised. Atahualpa accepted Christianity and was to be strangled instead of being burned alive.

No doubt, Francisco Pizarro, on this August morning in 1533, recalled Cortes' tactics in Mexico. Seven years before, during a military expedition against Honduras, Cortes was advancing through the jungle with a prisoner, the last Aztec king Cuautemoc. He had already subjected him to torture by roasting the soles of his feet to make him disclose the hiding-place of his treasure; but this was an old memory, and since then Cuautemoc had been baptised, and he was now called Ferdinand after his conqueror and godfather. However, Cortes mistrusted him, for he was accused of conspiring against the Spaniards, and so, far away in the country and without trial, Cuautemoc was hanged. The betrayal that Cortes had perpetrated in Mexico was about to be repeated in Peru. Pizarro was godfather to the Inca and had given him his name. It was indeed Francisco Atahualpa who came forth from prison to his execution.

There was a vast crowd in the great square, but of the common people, since the chiefs and military leaders refused to be present at their master's execution. As the king appeared, a shudder passed over the Indians assembled there, and they prostrated themselves on the ground. The son of the Sun advanced into the midst of his subjects, who lay prostrate and trembling with holy terror. Would they not rise in hatred and destroy with hands and fists this group of bearded murderers gathered round the single stake which had been erected in their midst? But they did not even raise their faces from the earth. It was their very soul which was being snatched from them and which went forth to die. Those spirits of thunder, lightning, and earthquake which they worshipped were all equally silent. The incredible silence was suddenly shattered by the strident call of the Spanish trumpets. The Inca must die, and with him the soul of the Inca people. Pizarro gazed at this mass of humanity, like corpses on the field of battle. Could these be men? the men of the Inca Empire with its organised life and its expression of the great Inca genius? The answer was that there was only one man, the man before him, Francisco Atahualpa.

The chaplain spoke to the king in a low voice, giving him friendly comfort at the moment of death, talking of the peace of Christ, of eternal life, for this was the formula for the mysterious passing on, the final open sesame. But these words came from another world—our world—where, even to the end of life, love strives to soothe the already numbered beatings of a human heart. The Spaniards knew how to kill. They had knowledge of love and death, and the marriage of the two at the last was one in which they excelled, if only one could understand the words! But Atahualpa was deaf to his executioner's tongue; he was entirely alone. He interrupted the priest and addressed Pizarro, 'Care for my children'.

The executioner led him to the stake and bound him to it. The rope was passed round his neck. Pedro Pizarro, the secretary, noted in his report, 'The Spaniards who stood around him recited a credo for his soul, and the king was quickly strangled'.[1]

The very day of the execution, Estete, De Soto, and their companions returned from their mission. They found Pizarro in a dark mood and wearing a felt hat as a sign of mourning. 'You have done an evil thing', cried Miguel de Estete. 'You should have awaited our return. There is not a single warrior in the country, and we have received friendly treatment everywhere'. The Governor, overcome with grief, exclaimed, 'I was deceived'. Amongst those whom he accused of this deceit was the treasurer, Riquelme, the envoy of the Council for the Indies. It was necessary to accomplish this crime to enforce the authority of the political agent. This man was not amongst the judges, and he has passed unrecorded in historical accounts, but he was undoubtedly responsible for more massacres than the conquerors themselves. He was plotting whilst the others fought. He was also a coward : he wanted to abandon Pizarro when he was in sight of the arid lands of the Peruvian coast. It was indeed he who directed the conquest politically. He should have listened to the advice of Ferdinand de Soto and sent Atahualpa to Spain. Why did he prefer to have him executed? Pedro Pizarro recorded the reason : 'With Atahualpa dead, all knowledge of the hidden treasure died with him'.

The threat of Spain was no vain one. She exacted much gold from the Conquistadors, but she also supervised their actions as far as she could. When Charles the Fifth learned of the Inca's death he reproached Pizarro. 'The death of Atahualpa, a man of high degree, has much displeased me, especially because it was the result of a court decision'. But those who arranged the trial at Cajamarca had defeated true justice. However these rude soldiers paid for their excesses. Bid them farewell, for the time has come to abandon them to their fate. We shall continue with the story of the living, the story of the men who built the Inca Empire. And the soldiers, despite their courage, would be uneasy travelling companions.

Francisco Pizarro died at the hand of an assassin in his palace at Lima.

Diego de Almagro was strangled in prison at Cuzco.

---

[1] The Indians of Cajamarca, after this, celebrated the memory of the death of Atahualpa. At the beginning of the 18th century the traveller, Frézier, was present at this feast, during which the natives, in ancient dress, bore images of the Sun in procession to the place of execution.

Almagro, his son, was executed four years after the death of his father.

Gonzalo Pizarro, the Governor's brother, was executed.

Carvajal was hanged and quartered, Garcia de Alvarado assassinated . . . the list is not complete.

In the book which slipped from Atahualpa's hand on to the ground where he died, the Conquistadors could have read this warning : 'He who lives by the sword shall perish by the sword'.

Fig. 6. The death of Pizarro.

PART TWO

□

CHAPTER I

ONCE UPON A TIME

At Cuzco in the 16th century, with the historians who reveal to us the ancient past of the Indians

□

A s dawn rose on Cuzco, the shadow of the high summits lingered a moment on the city, as if to allow nocturnal wanderers to regain their homes. Then the mountains drew aside the last veil of dawn, and Cuzco was bathed in light. A cock crowing, a bell ringing . . . was this indeed the heart of the Inca Empire? This was the capital city on this summer morning of the year 1550. For fifteen years the Conquistadors had been in occupation, but the daily birth of the sun was still observed by the sacristans and the backyard birds. The paved or cobbled streets were still almost empty, save for an Indian who trotted by with bare feet and a bent back. He turned at right angles and disappeared down a similar street which had a channel running down the middle between grey stone walls. The monotony of this chequer-board city was bewildering—even the heart of it was square. Once this vast bare arena was a market, a forum, and a place of worship where, at the summer solstices, the crowd waited for the sun with the same emotion that the French courtiers awaited the king's arising. Now, three monks crossed the square and hastened towards a chapel, probably to say mass for some Conquistador executed by his companions. But there appeared to be no church; only four Inca palaces with austere lines marked out the square. Spanish tools had scarcely been able to cut into the foundations to place a mud clock-tower on the Indian granite.

This was now a half-breed city, and as such it appeared in the morning sunshine. Certainly it still retained the shape of a puma, whose head was the fortress of Sacsahuaman towards the north, and whose tail was the stream of Vilcamayo winding across the plain. In addition all the buildings were of Inca construction, with long houses built of irregular polygonal blocks of stone, solidly placed like the palace of King Roca on the square, or built with the elegance of the last period of the Empire, of carved, polished stones

67

placed in a regular design. But later, on the site of a royal house 160 yards long, the cathedral was built, and above the Temple of the Sun the Dominicans erected their monastery.

The walls of the capital city showed the political policy of the conquerors—a mixture of old and new. The builders kept the Inca foundations, but from eye-level upwards, the Spanish tradition appeared. The shields of the old Spanish nobility were engraved above the finest doors, and in the adobe walls, made of mud rubble set on the stone foundations, they cut windows and attached pillared balconies. Air and light from the street entered houses which for centuries had only interior courtyards.

There were still one hundred thousand Indians in Cuzco, but the town belonged to the Conquistadors, and they each wanted their own section with its church and manorial residence. The Inca's immediate family was confined in the palace of Colcampata, which had a beautiful outlook, but apart from this pleasant courtesy towards the hereditary rulers, the Spaniards organised the city to suit their own convenience. Guitars joined with Indian flutes and drums, and the dances of Andalusia mingled with Andean dances from the high plateaux to reproduce, in the course of many evenings, an entirely new harmony. The little Indian musicians played up to their conquerors' nostalgia for home, and the girls from the Cordilleras took care of the rest. The vicuña robes and jaguar skins, so soft to Inca feet, made wedding couches fit for conquerors! And many of the children, with their sun-kissed skin and gentle features showing a half-way meeting of the races, were baptised. The Indians thought that their Mother Earth would triumph in the end and the Andean blood would be the stronger by the time the children reached the age of ten or eleven. This was the age of the boy whose story follows.

In April, 1539, a son was born to the knight La Vega and an Indian lady, Isabelle Chimbu Ocllo, a member of the royal family and thought to be the grand-daughter of Tupac Yupanqui, the tenth king of the dynasty. The boy was then of high birth, but his name came down to posterity by other means, for he was Garcilaso de la Vega, half-breed chronicler and first South American historian. His father was first mentioned as arriving on the Pacific coast with Alvardo, and as having destroyed a collection of emeralds by testing their hardness by blows with a hammer, after the curious habit of the first explorers. Since then he had shown his mettle in the course of several campaigns, some against rebellious Indian tribes and some against his own compatriots, for the sharing of the Inca treasures had let loose civil war amongst the conquerors. Gonzalo Pizarro, the Governor's brother, had assigned to him certain lands near Cuzco, and La Vega was one of the eighty manorial lords of the capital city. He had the right to a modest palace, and he kept open house, entertaining between one and two hundred guests each evening, for he had the labours of thousands of peasants to maintain his revenues. So wealthy a man naturally sought an alliance with a girl of royal birth, and this was easy to accomplish, for the downfall of a monarchy always fosters a spontaneous increase of the aristocracy. La Vega chose the princess Chimbu Ocllo, and although he did not marry her, she bore him two children, of whom one was Garcilaso.

The early years of the future historian were those of the gilded youth of Cuzco at that time. He was present at his father's horse races and bull fights, for bulls were imported almost at the same time as the monks. He became a good horseman and learned to hunt stags and wild duck, though at the same time he received instruction in the art of politics. Examples of this were close at hand, for on the gallows in the square the severed heads of citizens whose opinions had differed alternated with the bodies of the hanged. When Garcilaso was five, the pressing problem was the choice between the Viceroy, Nunez Vela, sent by Spain, and the Conquistador, Gonzalo Pizarro. La Vega vacillated between the two, with varying fortune, for his enemies pillaged his house, and he indulged himself in a fusillade of bullets fired at close quarters as a reprisal. The child was more alarmed by the sight of a Spanish lady swinging at the end of a rope with her tongue out. His father no doubt told him that European customs were hardly more civilised, for Henry the Eighth of England had just died, Ivan the Terrible had just succeeded to the Russian throne, and Charles the Fifth was preparing a fifth war. Du Bellay, by contrast, had just published his *Defence and Illustration of the French Language,* but they could hardly have been aware of this in Cuzco. Garcilaso was brought up in the school typical of his age, with that slight time lag which fanaticism gave to the Spanish era. But with Chimbu Ocllo he found a gentleness which was not only maternal.

There was a tenderness of the past to which he owed half his being, and the Inca's history seemed to him humane and glorious compared with the bloody politics of the Conquest. Tyrants and all-powerful kings, like wars, no longer inspire fear when their age has passed—on the contrary they inspire pride, and old men and children are enchanted by them, preferring legend to true life. Chimbu Ocllo's friends were past officials of the Empire, followers of the legitimate king, and to whom Atahualpa was a usurper whom they held responsible for the occupation, with its dissolute customs and costly way of life. When the master of the house was away, the old noblemen avenged themselves for their misery by coming to eat maize grains and taste the traditional fermented drink, which the princess served to them in silver vessels. (At their own houses they ate from earthenware dishes, the only vessels that had not been stolen.) Garcilaso was present at these meetings and listened entranced to the stories about the appearances of Viracocha, to the wise sayings of King Pachacutec, and to tales of the victories of Yupanqui. During the day he learned from a qualified teacher what was known in Europe (where Copernicus had just died) about the moon. But at night the wonderful universe of the stars, so near to the land of the Incas, revealed other presences to him. He was told that the patches on the moon were made by the claws with which a love-sick wolf had mauled the goddess Killa. No doubt the heart of the young half-breed made a choice between official science and legend, but he learned also to play his part in life, for daily bread could not be assured only by the poetry of Indian beliefs. He was a true son of his period.

In 1560 he left his native land, but before his departure he visited the officer of justice, Polo de Ondegardo, a friend of the Indians. Ondegardo took him into a room in his house and showed him five mummies which he had saved from destruction. Here were the bodies of five dead Inca kings, crowned with turbans, and with circlets of gold where their eyes should have been. Garcilaso dared to touch the hand of the Inca Huayna Capac. Was he bidding farewell to his ancestors and promising never to forget them? He fought as a soldier in strange and incomprehensible lands, on behalf of John of Austria and Philip II, who exploited their adopted children even to the point of taking their life-blood. After thirty years he retired to Cordova and began to write the story of his youth, *Florida del Inca*. It was a short history of the period, describing what he himself had seen and what he had learned from the principal actors. On the one side were the Conquistadors, with their almost lion-like courage, their vanity, their cruelty in battle, yet so tenderly disposed towards their horses that they wept if one died; Don Quixotes who had left their Sanchos behind in the villages of Estremadura; and on the other side the mysterious Indians, strong as their native soil yet fragile as the mountain plants, despairing yet fascinated by their conquerors. Garcilaso's two worlds stifled each other in his history. As he also translated the love dialogues of the Hebrew writer Leon, it may be supposed that the Inca was follower of Plato. At last his great work appeared, the *Comentarios reales de los Incas,* under his complete signature, Garcilaso Inca de la Vega. This book is vital for learning about old Peru. It has been criticised, often with naïve severity, as if history was a mathematical science! Certainly his chronology is doubtful, his admiration of the genius of the Inca kings too passionate, and his facts rather tendentious. Garcilaso the writer had not properly appraised the results of his reading as a grown man. Of his literary masters he only showed certain influences: the subtlety of Seneca, the humanism of Petrarch, the search for truth in ideas and not in passing manifestations which the theory of Plato advised him. But such as it is, his book remains the best companion for those exploring the past history of the Incas. We can recognise the friendly voices and seek out the truth behind the emotion of an aged guide explaining the country of his ancestors.

We can compare other reactions. First that of the 'Stories' told by the officer of justice, Polo de Ondegardo, who discovered the five royal mummies in a convent and showed them to young Garcilaso. Ordered by the Viceroy of Peru to study the economic life of the ancient Empire, he became the archeologist of its administration and finances. It was not easy in a country which had no writing and where men took the place of official files. But he sought out the legends and sifted with some care the information he collected. But he became enthusiastic when describing the knotted cords of different colours by means of which the Incas recorded all forms of activity. He did not hide his sympathy with the Indians.

Another chronicler, Cieza de Leon, shared his feelings. He was a soldier who took an interest in human geography, passing by normal progression from roads to architecture and then to government. He arrived in America in 1534, at the age of thirteen, soon after the Spaniards entered Cuzco. When he was thirty-two, Cieza de Leon completed his *Crónica del Peru.* If books have their own aroma, his book exuded the cold air of the high plateaux and the sugary softness of the sheltered valleys. He loved the Cordilleras. It was the same in the case of Father Montesinos, who said he had crossed the Andes sixty times, being more interested in the legends of the past than in the petty cares of the present day. He was an imaginative seeker—almost too imaginative. But one cannot say this of another Jesuit, Barnabas Cobo, since at the age of seventeen, and entirely alone, he undertook to discover El Dorado, that country of the golden king whose mirage will doubtless dazzle our grand-children—one cannot destroy dreams! Cobo found treasures more interesting than the king with the golden beard. In his *Historia del Nuevo Mundo,* amidst a great mass of varied and often second-hand information, are observations on natural history which are agreeably accurate. The Jesuit had in fact glanced at the book of a great traveller, Juan de Sarmiento. Cobo had a good memory, and Sarmiento was a useful guide to him, especially as the latter was President of the Council for the Indies. Thus it was that he arrived at Cuzco in 1550 and Garcilaso's father must have entertained him at his table. In spite of his age and office, he was attracted by the Peruvian ladies, but his mind was perfectly clear when·he drew his picture of the Inca civilisation during its last period. The title of his book reveals its author's intentions—*Relación de la sucesión y gobiernos de los Incas.*

This benevolent attitude towards the people and objects of the past was shared by all the Spanish chroniclers of the time except certain courtiers of the Viceroy, Francisco de Toledo. Had it not been for certain fanatical writers assembled at his court, this dull and conscientious man would have left behind to posterity only a list of fallen heads—among them Amaru Tupac, the last of the figure-head kings in the service of the conquerors. These writers were of the Toledo school, of whom Gamboa was the best representative. His *History of Peru* is a sorry book, but it is interesting for that very reason. It reflects the secret thoughts of the supporters of war against the Indians and of those who profited by slavery, which·was carried on under the legal cover of the *encomienda.*[1]

Throughout the ages men have sought an ideology to explain their actions and to condemn those whom they have exploited. But it must be recognised that this was not fundamentally a Spanish

---

[1] System by which Indian labour was allowed to be used in return for religious instruction and for 'protection'.

custom. On the contrary, the Council for the Indies listened attentively to one man who made his love for the Indians his life's work and who contributed to knowledge of the Incas by his book *De las antiguas gentes del Peru*. This was Bartholomew de Las Casas, who was the son of a settler in the Caribbean Islands. He sold his lands, set free his slaves, and became a priest. Until his death, both in the colonies and at the Spanish court, he struggled against the abuses of the Conquest. He even obtained new legislation which suppressed the *encomiendas* and assured to the natives, theoretically at least, the same rights as the subjects of the crown. His short account of *The Destruction of the Indies* was not only a condemnation of a system of exploitation and death, but opened a new horizon for his age—that of the equality of the Indians in the sight of God, the law, and their fellow men. For this reason Las Casas is one of the best of our fellow travellers.

We shall also keep brief company with an Indian about whom little is known except that he called himself a king's grandson. His name was Felipe Inca Tupac Yupanqui, and he protested about Huaman Poma and his manuscript called *Nueva crónica y bien gobierno*. It cannot be denied that here was a novel account, for it was in a form in which Indian and Spanish words were intermingled, and he recounted like a clever child the long sad story of his people from the time of Adam and Eve. Huaman drew better than he wrote, and his illustrations are a precious witness, for he puts on record the setting of ancient times.

We now have a goodly collection around us: a bishop, missionaries, a soldier, a high official, a clerk, a true writer, an artist, and since a Judas must always be present in a human undertaking, the courtier Gamboa. We shall complete our company with a settler, Juan de Betanzos, once an interpreter and later married to Pizarro's widow (sister to Atahualpa). He adds a work to our collection, *Suma y narración de los Incas*, which turns our interest towards the Aymaras, the southern neighbours of Peru. Of course we shall encounter on our way travellers in other centuries who by reason of their own choice, their scholarship, or because they have been sent by scientific bodies, have set out along the roads to the Cordilleras. These have above all investigated ruins and tombs, and the silent replies the stones have given to their questions will add to the historians' accounts.

Let us return to the gathering we left earlier on, in the house of

La Vega at Cuzco. There was present that night a very old man, a retired Inca general. He had fought under Huayna Capac and was amongst those privileged to be present at his death-bed. Garcilaso listened to him with great respect and even risked asking him a question.

'How do you know our history so well, Uncle Cusi-Hualpa? Could you tell me who was the first of our kings and how he reigned?'

The Inca, delighted by his nephew's manners, replied, 'You must know that throughout the length of our land there was once nothing but mountains and precipices covered with briars and thorns. The men were like animals, without government, religion, or fixed dwellings. They ate grass, fruits, roots, and often human flesh. Those who did not always go naked covered themselves with the skins of animals, bark from trees, or with leaves. They had no wives, but took the first woman they met'.[1] Cusi-Hualpa's voice died away. No doubt the wind swept it up to the empty, cold Cordilleras, which were so dark that without the stars no one could have distinguished them from the black night.

[1] *History of the Incas,* by Garcilaso de la Vega.

CHAPTER II

EARLY CIVILISATION

The Cordilleras of the Andes–The tribes seek a good land–The Urus settle near Lake Titicaca–The supreme god of Chavin–Dr. Tello unfolds the story of the first Peruvian Empire

□

A CONDOR gliding above the rock where its young are calling loudly. . . A humming bird beating its wings in front of a wild lily. . . An aloe in flower near the snow-line. . . A desert plateau swept by the wind ... Suddenly a ravine, red with porphyry, like an open wound. . . A warm spring flowing at the height of Mont Blanc. . . A fertile plain and a lake, close to jagged peaks. . .

A traveller in the Andes can never stop marvelling at the diversity and contrast of the Cordilleras. One day perhaps he will be kept

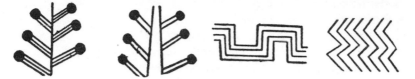

Figs. 7 and 8. Decorative motifs from Indian pottery

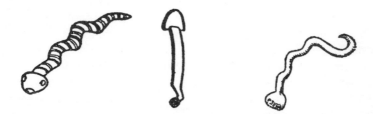

prisoner by a storm sweeping through the forest; the avalanches will crumble the line of the summits and a new mountain will rise up in their place. The Cordilleras seem to him to wear the enigmatic appearance of the Indian inhabitants, whose real strength is concealed. Chasms of subterranean light, mineral-bearing outcrops, and rocks yielding up their precious stones all seem to be mani-

75

festations of the true spirit of this Andean world. The traveller is anxious to know how, in olden times, the Indians depicted the Cordilleras on their materials or pottery. The decoration on Inca vases, with their Grecian shapes, showed that the ancient Peruvians did not represent their country as they did the simple forms of men and beasts. They drew elaborate, formalised pictures in which the outlines were confused with their own emotions.

At the warmer levels grew trees with sweet fruits, then bushes loaded with farinaceous seeds, cactus with red and white blossoms, heathers, tough pasture grass, miniature flowers, modest as daisies, and then towards the heights on the edge of the glaciers were lichens. At this altitude man's only companions were the condors and llamas. The dry air, the cold and the cosmic rays restricted animal life, and it was only on descending to the lower, damper slopes that pumas, stags, skunks or hares were found. Snakes were lower still, on the border of the tropical belt.

In early times, the fauna indicated the pattern of the Andean world. Fossilised bones and imprints show traces of the great horses of Ecuador, of armadillos as big as dinosaurs, and of a few mammoths which had found their way from Asia. Well-preserved skins and unexpected traces of their excrement were even left behind by these lazy giants of the south. Did these prehistoric species last on until the dawn of more recent times? Obsidian arrowheads found in the skeletons indicated the presence of hunters.

Our friends the historians had their ideas about the settlement of America, but they smack of the ecclesiastical. Nevertheless, consider the opinion of a monk, a doctor of theology named Antonio de la Calancha, whom Barnabas Cobo met at Lima at the end of the 16th century. He began by saying that in all justice Peru ought to be called Pizzarrina, but in spite of this Italian comedy introduction, Antonio was a considerable personage. He wrote that those who peopled the American continent were the descendants of Japhet, Noah's third son. They were Tartars—a race given to conquest and the settlement of far-off lands. After a learned dissertation taken from Saint John Chrysostom and Saint Augustine, comparing the wanderings of Gentiles and Indians, Father Antonio recorded a native tradition that the first men came from the north. He says that it was well known that Estotilandia or Cape Labrador was only separated from the country of the Tartars by eight or ten leagues of sea, and that from Estotilandia to Chile there extended continuous dry land. The monk had pretty solid notions of geography. And so he may be pardoned for having abandoned himself to a certain explorer's enthusiasm as follows.

'From Tartary to Estotilandia, 90 degrees from east to west, may be 1,575 leagues. From this point Lima is 90 degrees from north to south, which totals in all about 3,150 leagues. By travelling seven leagues a day, the journey from Tartary to Lima could be done in 450 days, about one year and three months. Even if delayed by the difficulties of the march, the Tartars could have arrived in Lima in a comparatively short time'.[1]

If we admit that four or five centuries would have sufficed, we might be nearer to—or further from—the truth. The route of Asiatic migrations by the Behring Strait, to which Calancha's account refers, is now classic. It remains to discover when the tribes first attempted this passage. Perhaps they were already on the march fifteen thousand years ago, driven from Asia by some cataclysm. Some came from Tibet, some from China, and others from the southern shores of the Pacific. The earliest of these migrants had a long skull; the more recent, from the Pacific coast, a wider skull. This description of these first men is the single secret yielded by American soil. One can only imagine a race of thick-set people with broad shoulders, yellow or copper-coloured skin, almost beardless, but with long black hair.

It is true that one can only build a picture in imagination, for these millions of men, moving across the earth for thousands of years have left, as proof of their presence, here and there only some arrowheads and scrapers, some grinding stones and mortars. Thus one can only guess at the activities of their daily life: men cooking their food on open-air hearths by putting it on heated stones or by throwing red-hot pebbles into gourds to make broth. These cunning cooks lived near the Pacific Ocean in the Viru valley to the north of Peru. They dwelt in caves hewn out of sheltering rocks, grew beans, pimento, and cotton, and fished in the waters of the Pacific. At home they wore clothes made from bark and mended their nets with needles fashioned from bones. Perhaps they sang or told stories, but the laughter of our cave-dwelling ancestors has not come down to us. Those living on the Peruvian coast ended up in a hole in the sand, where they were placed after death.

But during this time, other races from Asia, and tribes who sailed

[1] *Crónica moralizada,* by Father Antonio de la Calancha.

from Polynesia and Australia took possession of the continent. They passed along the empty coast or penetrated the plains to the east. How can we follow these nomads through country still virgin, but which, thanks to them, slowly ceased to be the world of the third day of the creation? Where can we fix the first meetings between the migrants from the north with the inhabitants of the south? Their first struggles, their first embraces? Here and there an enquiring finger pulled from the soil knives made from shells, spears with saw-teeth, objects shaped from lava, and even pearls set in bird bones. Happily it only took a man's skull side by side with that of a humming bird to mark with a cross the silent map of pre-history. In Lagoa Santa in Brazil, the caves of Palli Aike near the Strait of Magellan, and the grotto of Alangasi on the equator, possibly the most ancient centres of population, whole peoples halted for a night or a century.

In the virgin forest there was nothing—or rather nothing could be seen but the infinite roof of the trees and the enormous ditches which carried away the water from the swamps. But the people we are seeking were there, wandering, desperate, naked. What destiny had brought them like a herd from the ice of Alaska to the warm mud of the Amazon? During their journey nothing had stopped them. They went on advancing through prairies and jungles, across to the southward to reach the Guianas, and from there they launched their canoes on the rivers flowing between soft walls of vegetation. They breasted the currents, eternally nomadic, seeking a good land. From generation to generation they were left as a heritage the obsession of finding a country where they could end their exhausting march, reunite the tribe, and live an organised life. They travelled blindly towards the mountains, building huts of foliage, modelling clay, clearing the bush, and pushing sticks into the soil so that they could take root. They planted, and they shared their harvests; they set snares and shared their game. At night they recounted the stories of their grandparents which would pass into legend the day they found somewhere to settle at last. Then they set off again, always towards the west, opening a path through the tenacious forest, decimated by snake bites, and, when they took to the great rivers, discouraged by a hostile sky full of clouds and storms. Generations passed, and one after another, like the beat of an oar, they exhausted themselves. Would the day never break fresh and clear from this permanent forest dawn?

However, a few managed to free themselves. They saw first of all the line of a hill; then they climbed the Cordilleras and found themselves 12,000 feet up on a desert plateau. Snowy summits bounded the horizon; grey water rippled in a cradle of rushes— this was Lake Titicaca,[1] an expanse so vast that its boundaries could not be seen. Was this the heart of the universe?

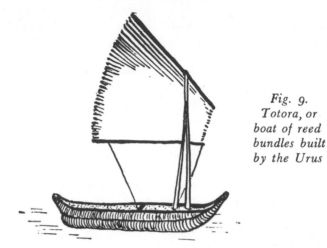

Fig. 9.
Totora, or
boat of reed
bundles built
by the Urus

The Indians who, like other men, sought a harmony of sun and water found here a situation which pleased them. To them the favourable signs were the nearness of the stars, the extremes of heat and cold, which meant the near presence of sun and moon, a land without wild beasts, without thorns, and with fresh water teeming with fish. The thin air was an expected liability from which it was impossible to escape. None of the races who reached the Andes ever willingly sought other lands to settle.

During the centuries the new arrivals took the name of Uru or Kotsuns; but their true origin was the Arawak race, of whom there remain only a few tribes scattered throughout the Amazon basin, and who, dispersed by years of travel, hunt with blow-pipes, fish with poisoned lines, and maintain the necessities of life by palm growing. Their brothers, the Urus, first secured their existence by

[1] Altitude: 11,436 feet. Area: 7,000 square miles. Length: 140 miles. Average width: 56 miles. Greatest depth: 716 feet. Temperature of water at 60 feet, 11 degrees centigrade (Doctor J. Vellard). According to Garcilaso de la Vega, Titicaca means the 'Lake of Lead'. According to P. Sanjines, 'The mountain of the wild cat (or jaguar)'.

using the reeds which grew on the edge of the lake, mixing them with mud to build their houses, and stretching and plaiting them to make a roof, a door, or a bed. Their boats were called by the name of this plant, totora.[1] Two huge reed bundles bound together formed the hull, and they travelled by means of a sail, a simple straw curtain, or by means of a pole, a precious stick cut from distant outskirts of the forest.[2] This Amazon technique was adapted to the lake in the Cordilleras. To catch fish, the Urus beat the water and guided the fish towards a double line of reeds which they had erected at an angle, where huge landing nets closed over the rustling scales. In the same way as in the forest clearings, where the Arawak women split the palm leaves to make string and rolled the threads across their thighs, the Urus treated the grass fibres of the high plateaux. They made string nets with which they captured water birds at dawn, whilst still benumbed with cold. They dried and smoked game to prevent decay, but their favourite method of cooking was by stuffing and baking food in underground ovens heated by red-hot stones. Later they planted quinoa and soon could plunge their hands into a soft flour. The totems they had preserved all through their long wanderings—snakes, monkeys and jaguars—protected them in the Andes as they had done in the virgin forest. They maintained that they alone had been spared when an earthquake had devastated the region of Lake Titicaca. An old man on the lake shore said, 'We are not men, we are older than men'.

In a valley to the south of the high plateau can be seen the remains of the oldest Andean civilisation: heads of pumas and jaguars carved in stone.[3] The eyes are hollowed out, or at times merely indicated, on blocks of red sandstone or volcanic tufa; the llamas are recognisable by their almond-shaped eyes. Alongside these animal motifs, a human head, almost square, with eyes and mouth also cut at right angles, is suggestive of an attempt to fuse the human and the feline. Everywhere the Indians express their desire to make the human being share the mysteries of a nature where everything is god-like save man himself. It is difficult to decipher the meaning of the stones at the period we are considering. Incidentally, how long ago was this? A thousand years before

[1] Totora: *scirpus totora* (Kunth).
[2] D'Orligny, in 1830, estimated that there were 1,000 Urus still alive. In 1927, Alfred Métraux counted less than 100. In 1950, Dr. Vellard counted only 12 pure-bred Urus.
[3] Cf. A. Métraux, *Journal des Americanistes*, Vol. XXVII.

Christ? The people settled on the Pacific coast had already a developed way of life, perhaps more brilliant. The Andes were forbidding and secretive.

Cieza de Leon was not of this opinion, for he affirmed that there was already a huge town on the shores of the great lake. Tiahuanaco, with its monolithic architecture, at an altitude of 12,000 feet on a desert plain, its huge staircase leading to a palace, was a subject for wonder. But we must not let ourselves be led astray. We cannot admire this Tiahuanaco of which the Spanish historian speaks, for his compatriots tore down tons of stone from it to build their own houses. We shall visit it later, when the armies of the fourth Inca king, Mayta Capac, came to subdue the tribes of the high plateau. Ten centuries before Christ, without a doubt, there were to be found at Tiahuanaco only rectangular buildings half-buried in the earth. The inner sides of the blocks of sandstone of which the walls had been built were polished, and above the columns could be seen the heads of feline beasts.

A thousand kilometres to the north of Lake Titicaca, an immense temple spread over the foot of a mountain; the near-by village was called Chavin. We may regard these ruins with respectful incomprehension through the eyes of Cieza de Leon in 1548, or of Antonio Espinoza in 1624. The latter wrote that the temple was one of the most famous, comparable with Rome or Jerusalem. But avalanches continued to fall upon these stones which men had carved. When the explorers of the last century were at Chavin, no one imagined that the face of ancient Peru would blossom forth under their hands. The Italian Raimondi and the Frenchman Wiener were at Chavin, the former to excavate a stela and the latter to make sketches. An Indian revealed the secret and we shall meet him later. At Chavin the face of ancient Peru, lightly touched by time, has recently been disclosed, fresh in spite of its 3,000 years.

On the slope which leads down to the river Puccha, huge platforms had been erected. The outer walls were of rectangular blocks of stone, polished and placed one on the other in such a way that the whole had the solid appearance of all Andean buildings. But on the top of the façade the cornices reproduced the features of condors, jaguars, and snakes. At the centre of the principal monument, fantastic heads were carved on the wall. Here is a reproduction of one of the strangest of beasts :

Fig. 10 (above).
Wall carving
from Chavin

Fig. 11 (right).
Carving from
Chavin

Farther away, a staircase of flagged stones led to the upper platform, and chapels or sacred compartments opened off a terrace. It
was there, between the colonnades of burned earth, that the rites of
the cult took place. The channels cut from the altars indicated the
nature of the sacrifices, and the victims' blood flowed to a sculp-
tured stela and poured over the face of a feline deity.

At Chavin the jaguar is everywhere: on bas-reliefs and obelisks,
and carved into the outer walls, side by side with the heads of birds
and snakes. These three animal shapes are humanised, for although
the Indian deities could not be men, the Indians, in their temples,

were in touch with supernatural forces and endeavoured to mingle their own features with those of the beasts whom they revered as their ancestors. In the virgin forest the tribes set up animal totems with geometrical patterns spread out over their bodies. In the Cordilleras they carved them on stone: birds with nostrils in their beaks, like human noses, while their feathers, hollowed out in deep wrinkles, sometimes had snakes at their tips—snakes with round eyes and triangular tongues darting from their jaws. There were also jaguars, usually with long-drawn-out muzzles and elliptical eyes. But one detail was found in almost all the heads—the croco-

Fig. 12.
Carving from
Chavin

diles. These humanised animals at Chavin had huge teeth sticking out of their mouths, and this sign of original hunger became an obsession.

Our historians say that once upon a time the people of the Cordilleras ate human flesh. The appearance of these heads, all ready to devour, leaves no doubt that the origin of their devilish taste was divinely inspired! The supreme god Onkoy is a dragon, carved on the central obelisk of the temple; he synthesises the Chavin religion. Connected with the stars by his association with the constellation of the Pleiades, Onkoy is a hybrid, both male and female, half feline and half reptile. He is pictured ready to spring. But while his head is a single mass, fierce, watchful and satiated, his body is made up of a mysterious digestive world. The crocodile's gastric tube, with pointed teeth, is the framework of the body; the back, which must be seen from above, reveals only one recognisable shape, a human with two arms; one arm rests against the first of ten subsequent figures which follow down to the dragon's tail. What is their meaning? Those who have seen the Mexican codices and know that the Indian genius tends to express itself in a similar way throughout the migrations of its peoples, refer to the pictorial records of the age and to the explanation given by soothsayers. The crouching man may be the priest, the future Calparicoc of the Incas. The other motifs which make up the dragon may be the heads, eyes, and other organs. The rear impersonates the crocodiles, crowned with a moon. Those with four-fingered paws, with human nails, are in their turn overlooked by heads which are watchful and

Fig. 13. Carving of the god Onkoy at Chavin

with many teeth. The forepaws are feline; the rear look like those of serpents. They reach after the products of a warm, sunny land: manioc, cotton and pimento. Above the head, snakes seem connected with the deity. And out in front are three animals darting ahead as messengers or spirits—the cat, the bird, and the fish.

The whole of nature is renewed in the graven idol on the obelisk at Chavin. The year through, the sun plays around it, and when the summer solstice arrives, the Pleiades make a brief appearance in the eastern night sky, and the dragon plays its part in measuring off the days. It materialises time. Like all men of olden times, the people of the Cordilleras were affected by cosmic phenomena and by the unchanging laws of the universe—unchanging, and for that very reason infinitely above all human activities. They ordered their life to the pattern of an eternal life, always trying to humanise it, almost to render it familiar, and thus hand it on to future generations. Perhaps one day we shall be able to decipher these figures which are at present hieroglyphics and where man and deity are mingled, and explain these eternal truths.

However, the Chavin tribesman was not only the enigma of a deified universe. He was equally an artisan—certainly a very humble artisan, limiting his personal tastes to the fashioning of small objects such as mortars, dishes or boxes. He made them from alabaster, onyx, turquoise or other precious stones. Finely chiselled with a graver, these objects reveal a geometric fancy, and also (why not?) a tendency towards art for art's sake. There are, too, gold plaques carved with snakes' heads, but this metal was little used as yet. Pottery was easier to decorate. On a black or grey background of baked clay, linear designs were chiselled with much skill. The farther one goes from the temple, following in space and time the spread of this culture, the freedom of expression of the artists becomes more evident, until a sort of humour is displayed in the representation of mythological beings. Of course it is in the tombs that the best-preserved pieces of pottery are found.

It is not possible to say which among the inhabitants of Chavin had the right of individual burial. To judge by the tomb found at the foot of the temple of Kuntur Wasi, which is dedicated to the worship of a double deity, bird-serpent, the dead belonging to the ruling class seem to have been well treated. The body was seated, with the legs folded back, and surrounded by six discs of beaten gold with reptilian motifs, by thirty-two small rectangular plaques also of gold, and with a necklace and some turquoises. Beside him, within reach of his hand, a cup of baked clay must have contained provisions for the long journey. All the same it is difficult to picture the dead man, for he disintegrated into dust. But his thousands of neighbours who lie in the earth awaiting interrogation may perhaps provide more definite information about the strange past of the Chavin civilisation. It may not be the most ancient form of known life in the Cordilleras of the Andes, but it is the most complete and the most representative of the life of the first Peruvians—and also the most extensive.

The man who tells us this is an Indian, an Indian of the present day, clad in black, discreet, and showing only by his flashing eyes the warmth of his feelings. He led more than fifty scientific expeditions across his country of Peru, founded six anthropological and architectural museums, and for the one he personally directed he acquired more than 82,000 objects. His name is Julio Tello. The author met him in 1941, six years before his death, and the very year of his last exploration of Chavin. Without him we should travel very uncertain ways and be ignorant of the essential origins of the Andean world. It has been said of Tello that like the Incas, he made knowledge a miracle of intuition. One can say that he gave the whole of his life to his love for the Indians of his race and country. 'Their aspirations', he said, 'they have buried deep in their hearts; aspirations proper to any human race, whether savage or civilised'. Ever since he was ten years old, when he gazed wondering at trepanned skulls, he always produced excellent reasons for the Peruvian people to be proud of their ancestors. Chavin was the greatest of these reasons. The first time he went there he discovered a monolith fifteen feet high, on which the supreme deity was carved. This was the beginning of the explanation of a whole world by means of the sun!

The Chavin culture is the most ancient pre-Columbian culture of Peru, he stated. Starting from its centre, east of the Andes, it spread to the limits of the virgin forest and then towards the coast and the Pacific Islands.

All the places on the adjoining map are stages in the spread of Chavin culture—all that have escaped volcanic eruptions, landslides, and human stupidity. Of course you will not find everywhere identical traces of a single way of life. Each region shows its own tendencies in style and art. At Kotosh, near the source of the river Huallaga, geometrical designs predominate, and these are the direct influence of the Amazon forest culture. At Kuntur Wasi pottery reaches a very advanced stage, and the ornamentation is in relief. On the coast, at Ancon, the people are clever basket makers, or carve small fetishes of gold. But the unity of the Chavin Empire can be defined by its deities, its sacred animals with their human characteristics, and by one permanent mark—those prominent crocodiles. The realm of Chavin was not war-like but religious. No building has ever been found to compare with their temples, as if their civilisation was an entirely priestly one.

In any case it was a very early civilisation. The individual played only a very restricted part. His life as a hunter or tiller of the soil, his dwelling, his recreations, have left scarcely any trace—the signs are lost. The Indian of olden times was ashamed of any thoughts contrary to divine laws, and he even apologised for having to make a hole in the earth to plant manioc or maize. Terror dominated the mind of man in a country where the altitude brought him near to

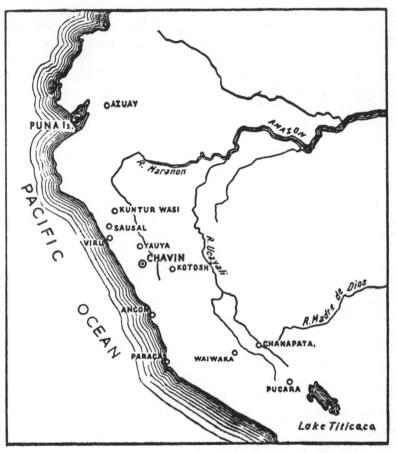

Fig. 14. The spread of Chavin culture

lightning and volcanoes and where the sun's rays caused delirium. What hope was there of survival, if not through the goodwill of the powers of nature? The Chavin people had brought their gods with them from the virgin forest—jaguars, monkeys, snakes, and the fish of the great rivers. In the Andes they added the condor, and prudently put the bird on some of their temples and made sacrifices to it. All their efforts tended towards producing a worthy setting for their deities—mountains were torn open, earth levelled, stones cut and engraved, and gold melted and carved. Let us hope the gods were there! They lived on the people who worshipped them, and drank their blood. Certainly some idols were endowed with human traits—but there was one strange feature: it seemed as if the Indians could imagine only a religion which had an insatiable hunger.

Julio Tello and the directress of the Archeological Museum at Lima, Rebecca Carrion, who carried out a similar work, both explain the ancient civilisations of their country quite simply. First an indigenous origin in the east; then three epochs of which the Chavin is the oldest and most widespread; then an intermediate period illustrated in the evolution of localised cultures, especially on the Pacific coast[1]; and finally the Incas. This logical and almost political classification accords little weight to influences outside Peru— those of the people of Central America, for example. But the final phase of the Incas seems like the crucible in which was fused all the diverse cultural elements of the intermediate period. It is a sort of logical concentration of centuries of effort, the creation of a genius which surmounts the ancestral terrors and gives opportunity to man's intelligence.

[1] Cf. Appendix.

CHAPTER III

THE CHILDREN OF THE SUN

Who is the god Viracocha?—The statue carved on the gateway of the Sun—The marvellous and delightful ancestors of the Incas—The intervention of the god—The sons of the Sun—Manco Capac, the first king, formulates the Indian way of life—Each month has its duties—The capital city

□

'WHERE art thou, our father, where art thou?'

For centuries the Indians, kneeling on the ground with their arms raised towards the sun, repeated this invocation. This prayer was directed to a higher being, the maker and guardian of the universe. Then one day the name of the god appeared in the prayers offered up by the Inca kings on feast days or on the eve of death.

> 'Viracocha, ruler of the universe,
> Man or woman,
> Lord of fertility,
> Who ever thou art, where art thou?'

Viracocha was the Peruvian conception of God, and he was called by a number of names, such as Kon Tiki Viracocha, or Kon Tiki Illac Viracocha. These numerous names for one deity no doubt resulted from the Incas' application of their technique of conquest to their religion; in the same way that they assimilated the knowledge of the people they conquered, they appropriated their gods to themselves. It was a considerable acquisition. At the end of the Empire, Kon Tiki Illac Viracocha represented a higher power than the simple Viracocha. But the latter remained the original deity.

The translation of this name has puzzled many scholars, but the most common rendering was 'the lake of foam', but it must be stressed that the riddle remains unsolved. Illac means lightning, and each person can imagine for himself the interpretation which the Indians gave to the combination of water, storm, and lightning. But the linking of the two words Kon Tiki invokes the imagination. Our Norwegian friends who crossed the Pacific on a raft regard Tiki as the sun. But Tiki is a Polynesian god, and so far there is no proof that he was of American origin. The two words Kon and Tiki belong to different languages and to people who are far removed from each other. Kon means sun among the Chimus on the north-west coast of South America, while Tiki comes from the language of the Aymaras, who live in the Cordilleras near Lake Titicaca. Possibly the simple explanation is that the Incas absorbed first of all the word Tiki at the time of the Aymaras, and then Kon when the Chimus surrendered. Moreover, the historian Zarate has told us the story of Kon the Chimu god. He was a son of the Sun and the Moon, different from ordinary mortals since he had 'neither skin nor bone', and came from the north to create the world. His subjects were disobedient, and to punish them he forbade the rain to fall, allowing only certain rivers to flow from the high mountains so that the region should not become entirely desert. However another and more powerful god came from the south and drove Kon out—he fled on the waves and never returned. The conquering god was Irma-Pachacamac, 'saviour' of the world, and he in his turn became associated with Viracocha when the Incas became masters of the coast of Peru.

The chroniclers agree that the cradle of the true Viracocha lies on Lake Titicaca and that he came forth from the waters to create heaven and earth and certain human beings. This would have been successfully accomplished had there been light. But as men struggled vainly in the darkness, they quarrelled, and to punish them—this obsession of gods to chastise their creatures!—Viracocha turned them into stones and went back to his lake. After a period of meditation, he assumed a less uncompromising attitude and came forth from the water a second time. He created the sun and moon and a new race of human beings capable of ruling themselves, or rather of being ruled, since he gave them a ruler.

One can still see today the figure of the god Viracocha amongst the ruins of Tiahuanaco, engraved on the monolith which is called the gateway of the Sun. This gateway of the Sun stands in the midst of a desolate plain. The monument is of one large block almost intact, standing nine feet high and twelve feet wide. However, the visitor who is more than about four feet in height must bow his head to pass through the central opening. Up to this height the uprights are smooth, but above, a frieze extends across almost the whole width. One feels an urge to touch the projections and hollows of the stone with one's fingers. In the thin air of the high plateau, contact with this mass of granite takes one back to the time when the sculptors' chisels created the image of the god. For it is indeed he who is the principal motif of the monument. He is represented as a jaguar in a very much stylised and humanised form. The intention is clear and it is confirmed by other heads of

Fig. 15.
Carving of the
god Viracocha
on the Gate of
the Sun at
Tiahuanaco

felines and condors which surround and ornament the body of the god.

The other emblems crowding the figure on the monolith are inspired by cosmic forces: thunder and lightning in the hands, and sun rays spreading out round the head. More subtle still, the smallest incision in the stone interprets the faith of millions. The jaguar heads which with the suns form the deity's halo and give it such a sense of power, are crowned by a disc. The muzzle, shaped like a scroll or circle, is not a chance effect. The great American archeologist, Ralph Harcourt, has found the same outline on pottery, gold pieces, knife handles, materials and stones, and thanks to him we can resume our forgotten journeys. From Central America to the coast of Peru, and from there to the very heart of the Cordilleras, the characteristic of the scroll form for the nose has been transmitted from one race to another. It remains unexplained, but perhaps one day the story told by an Indian from the Amazon basin will provide a clue. For today the living Amazon basin withholds the key to the last of the Indian puzzles, and it is in the virgin forest that another detail of the face of the deity of Tiahuanaco is found: the tears, which are the symbol of rain and fertility. To sum up, from the Guianas to the Andes and throughout the Amazonian forest there exists a weeping deity whose tears are shaped, carved, or painted on the funerary urns of many tribes.[1] And thus the central figure at Tiahuanaco appears as the unification of all the Indian beliefs of a whole continent. The Incas knew and possibly worshipped this god even when they were still a small tribe living on the edge of the lake. When they returned to Tiahuanaco as conquerors several centuries later they found the idol intact.

Viracocha is the true god of the Incas, inseparable from their dynasty and Empire. He was already embodied in the name of the

Fig. 16.
Vari
Viracocha
runa,
as
pictured
by
Huaman
Poma

Inca ancestors whom the Indian Huaman Poma considered the first generation of Incas. According to the Indian, their first ancestors were called *Vari Viracocha runa,* or the 'viracocha men of the country'. These were incarnations of the god on earth, living amongst fierce wild beasts and apprehending only enough to turn their faces to the sun to pray. Next came *Vari runa,* or the 'country people', who increased for thirteen hundred years. They were a race of giants, clad in the skins of animals, and scratching the earth to set their plants. Next came *purun runa* or 'the people of the desert',

---

[1] *Comparative Archeology,* by Emile Wagner and O. L. Righetti. Buenos Aires, 1946. E. Wagner, a tireless French explorer, directed the Archeological Museum at Santiago del Estero, Argentina.

Fig. 17.
Vari
runa

Fig. 18.
Purun
runa

countless as the sand, as Huaman Poma says, and they went on increasing for 1,032 to 1,100 years. Huaman hesitates between the 32 and the 100, and finally, with a truly mathematical mind which does him credit, struck out the 32. Here then, for eleven centuries,

Fig. 19.
Auca
runa

the desert people built dwellings and worked with wool. Their wives were virtuous and there was *ni puta ni puto*.

The fourth group, *auca runa* or the 'warlike people', lasted, as would be expected, for the longest time, 2,100 years, building fortresses, seizing their neighbours' wives and devastating their plantations. Then they appointed a ruler in each village, became pious, and produced philosophers, astrologers and grammarians. They kissed on the mouth when they married, and evidently became a civilised people. According to Huaman Poma, the true founders of the dynasty came from this stem, and they were called *Tocay Capac* and *Pinay Capac*. These two persons also appear in the account given by another Indian, Santacruz Pachacuti. Now we are no longer in the age of mythology but have come to what is a matter of history. Legend is still strong but it is easier of explanation, and from the fog of marvels reality beckons.

Four brothers lived on an island in Lake Titicaca. Their names vary according to the historians. They are

Manco		Manco
Colla	or	Ayar cachi
Tocay		Ayar uchi
Pinau		Ayar auca

They can be considered as the same persons, and the eldest has the same name in both versions. We know nothing of the reasons for their presence on this island, but we do know what happened to them, thanks to the chroniclers. To be sure, we have to choose between several accounts, some by poets, others by theorists; the latter will suit the sceptical reader best.

The poets show no surprise at an apparition which we have no difficulty in recognising as the Sun, sent by the god Viracocha. He predicted that the four brothers would conquer numerous lands and would become great rulers. He said, 'Look on me as your father, proclaim that you are my children, and do not forget to pay me homage'. Then with a light thrust with his heel he flew up towards the sky. Barnabas Cobo maintains that the Incas' solar paternity was established in this way. From this time the four brothers became four communal chiefs struggling for power. They lived on a mountain, or more exactly in the cave of Tambotoco. From there they set out to find a fertile valley. On the way, the first brother was abandoned in a cave, and the second, according to the story of the survivors, was turned into stone. The third met the same fate later on, and Manco was left with his wife to rule the tribe.

There was also another poetic theme running through the adventures of Manco and his wife, Ocllo, who was also his sister. At the beginning the Sun designated them as his protégés. He offered them a golden staff, advising them to plant it at the spot where it would go in easily. 'The pair left Titicaca and went towards the north, testing the ground with the golden rod wherever they stopped. After travelling for a long time, they came at last to a place named Paracec Tambo, which means the Break of Day'. They were within a few leagues of the city of Cuzco. The Huanacauti valley showed itself amenable to the test with the golden staff. Manco then 'said to his wife (and sister), "It is here that the Sun, our father, wishes us to stop, and to obey him, we must gather together the people of this country"'. The style of the 18th century translator has been retained, for a better account could not be given of the way in which this Indian chose a territory for his tribe.

The theorists, always prone to consider the ancient gods as men with brains, eyes and common sense, are more ready to accept the account of the Indian Collas, who did not believe in the appearance of the Sun, but of a more powerful personage. This deity divided the world into four parts, which he then presented to four men whom he called kings. This was the confident belief of Cusi Hualpa, the old legitimist uncle of Garcilaso, who, it must be admitted, had a certain critical sense.

However, there is a more rational explanation of the origins of Manco and his wife, and one which is more suited to the spirit of our time. It appears in an account by the Indian Huaman Poma, who lived in the 16th century. The text is difficult to decipher, but a translation follows.

'Manco Capac had no known father. Because of this, he called himself son of the Sun *Yntip churin quillap nanan*'. Huaman explains as follows : 'Manco's mother was said to be a sorceress who held communication with demons and conversed with the stones, trees, mountains, and lakes'. Her name was Mama Uaca. Her reputation was somewhat notorious 'for she slept with any man she fancied and this deceit lasted for many years'. At this point the text is obscure. She appears to have married one of her own sons and had a child by him. On the advice of the devil, she did not acknowledge her offspring but gave him into the care of a wet-nurse, who brought him up in a cave. When he was two, she announced to the people that a young and all-powerful chief, son of the Sun and Moon, brother of the Shepherd's Star, had come forth from the place called Pacari Tambo and would rule over men. This was Manco. A second text by Huaman states quite simply that this astute woman 'married her first-born son Manco Capac Inca' and then herself took the name of Mama Ocllo. The family circle was thus made inviolate ! It is only necessary to alter the definition of the first royal pair and say Manco and his wife (and mother) instead of Manco and his wife (and sister)—a strange affair. If it were necessary to repeat and comment on the accounts of Ondegardo and Sarmiento, some revision would be called for. They speak of the presence of white, bearded men in very early times on the banks of Lake Titicaca. They are said to have built a huge city (Tiahuanaco) and taught the natives the advantages of the civilisa-

esk ynga crayno ĩoleelcuz̃o a camama

Fig. 20. The first Inca king, Manco Capac

tion of our Middle Ages. It is known that among the founders of American religions, Quetzalcoatl, the benevolent deity of the Aztecs, and Bichica, 'the royal cloak of light' of the Chibcha Indians of Colombia, had, according to certain Spanish chroniclers, fair skins, and the latter were bearded. But the more exact the information the natives are able to pass on about their past history, the more it becomes clear that the skin of the Mexican god returns to its original colour of copper-yellow. The interpretation given to primitive traditions which show traces of analogy with Christian forms of religion must equally be treated with reserve.[1] As far as actual knowledge goes, there is no reason for asserting that 'white men', bearded or not, had played any part in Indian life in South America before the arrival of the Spaniards. The obsession of certain writers with the idea of tall, fair, hearty men with clear eyes as the first globe-trotters of our civilisation arouses suspicion. We know this lighthearted tune too well. To suppose that Viracocha was a European, to allow him to intervene in the organisation of the Inca Empire, would result in adding a rather attractive legend, without foundation, to a history which already verges on fantasy. Let us return to Manco and Ocllo on their fertile alpine plain, nine thousand feet high.

Of all the Andean valleys, this was the richest and most sheltered. To east and west the mountain tops were not higher than fifteen thousand feet—a reasonable altitude in this region. To the north, the Anta plateau thinned out towards the Cordillera of Vilcapampa, which closed the horizon. It was lovely on these plains. The sun shone from May to September and favoured the cultivation of crops from the cooler regions, and the western roads led to warm valleys with their luxuriant produce. This pleasant land was inhabited already when Manco and Ocllo settled there. The chroniclers say that it was peopled by 'savages', but in reality the valley contained an agricultural race, peaceful and satisfied with its lot. They came from the Amazon forests, as did most of the Andean races, and they remained faithful to their traditional way of life. They were formed into tribes, each bearing its ancestor's name. Garcilaso describes them as 'worshipping plants, trees, mountains, and even wild animals'. If today we question the forest Indians, they say in their turn that they are the people of the tortoise, the

[1] Here is an example taken from the *Nueva Crónica* . . . 'The ancestors of the Incas of Peru knew of a god who was three in one'.

vampire, or of tobacco. The original idea is the same, for man needs protection, and there is no security away from the tribe.

Amongst these conservative races, the great genius of Manco and Ocllo was to proclaim themselves children of the Sun. Here was an ancestor infinitely superior to the totem deities of the Indians. The Iawas of the central Amazon[1] have recounted the legend of the birth of the Sun which enables us to understand this hierarchy easily. 'The planet at the beginning of all things', they say, 'was the moon. To save mankind from darkness the moon sent an animal on earth, endowed with a sacred power; this animal was the jaguar. His mission was to unite with a woman of the tribe, and the fruit of this union was an Indian. Then one day he stood by the hearth and was transported by the flames of the fire up to the sky, where he was transformed into the sun'. The gods could in this way breed men, but men who were immortal and destined to rejoin their celestial ancestors.

It was in this way that the Inca pair presented themselves to the people of the valley of Huanacauti. 'The "savages" gazed with astonishment at these two persons decked with ornaments given them by the Sun (the gold discs which the Incas affixed to their ears). They worshipped them from that moment'. It may be thought that Manco was really one of the tribal chiefs of these so-called 'savages', who had succeeded in extending his authority over the whole people. Even if the legends do not permit us to discover by what means he arrived, they certainly indicate that he was surrounded by celestial guarantees, and his kingship was strictly by divine right.

Manco, settled on the plain, undertook the conquest, or rather the organisation, of neighbouring villages. In this region the groups were of the Quechua tribe and also some Aymaras cut off from the main body of their people. 'They learned to cultivate the soil, to recognise the best vegetables, and to make use of the streams running through the valley. Ocllo, on her side, showed the women how to spin, how to card wool, and how to make materials for their clothing, and taught them to care for their houses'. This needful and practical approach, as described by the historians, was indeed the germ of the future Inca Empire. But for the time being, men's lives depended on the rhythm of the seasons.

[1] Cf. *Iawa, Peuple Libre,* by the same author, published by Amiot-Dumont, Paris.

When August came, the Indians sharpened the long spades which they used for tilling. Before going out into the fields they brought jars of maize wine, and fish or slaughtered sheep as offerings to their protective deities. When they had nothing to offer, the priest of the community sacrificed a young man or girl, and Huaman Poma states that they were buried alive. Then the men marched off into their fields and began to plough the furrows. The young women picked out the stones and turned under the sod; the old women brought refreshments. Ploughing and sowing were not drudgery, but a way of asking the goodwill of the Sun. Later on, even the Incas themselves handled spades in the gardens at Colcampata where the sacred maize was grown. Sacred or not, hard or soft, maize was the fundamental of Indian life. It was used for flour, bread, drink; and even the stalks, when green, secreted a delicious honey. On the slopes where maize would not grow they planted quinoa, whose flowers resembled the European blits; and above all they grew potatoes, large and small, bitter and sweet. Those who have tasted Chunu will remember the piquant flavour of this floury pulp, taken from the cold, high plains and preserved for months by exposure to the sun before being chewed on some feast day. The big, insipid potatoes were eaten with circumspection, for they rendered women sterile unless they clasped a talisman ring in their hands during the meal, to preserve them from harm. Other crops, such as beans, were harmless, and the valley of Huanacauti never allowed its inhabitants to die of hunger.

Could the Indians die of hunger? Those seen today, isolated on the plateaux, far from villages, are much poorer than the tribes subdued by Manco. Potato soup, a few grains of maize, and sometimes a strip of dried meat is sufficient for their daily needs throughout the year. Anything more they had was the result of chance experiments with a variety of plants, such as the aloe. On the slopes, the long spindles of the aloes burst forth like flames, and their pale green leaves were as precious as warmth to the Indians. The aloe seed disinfected wounds; boiled with its roots it was used as a tonic; mixed with maize liquor it was an intoxicant. It could be either vinegar or honey. The leaves, cleaned and dried, were used for fibre to make soles, or thread to sew clothing and to make nets for hunting birds. From the roots they made soap, and the women mixed it with other herbs to produce a dye, a disinfectant, or a reviver. They soaked their hair for two hours in the boiling liquid, lying on their backs, undergoing this small torture, whilst taking care to protect their necks from the fire. The aloe crept into the beauty secrets of the earliest women.

Then there was hunting. But the people of the valley had to go far to the south to catch ducks, coot, and herons, either by driving them into nets or by breaking their legs with the bolus—a weapon with three cords, similar to that used by the riders on the pampas to catch ostriches. The falcon was not yet trained and did not compete with the hunters. Game was rare, except for stags and llamas, and as soon as they could lay hands on the latter long-haired ruminant, they domesticated it not as a beast of burden but on account of its wool. The women then had something to spin and weave so that they could make tunics for their families.

This was the way the people of Manco and Ocllo lived. It seemed that no law was necessary to regulate such a simple existence. Their only rule up to that time had been to share the sun's produce amongst the members of the tribe. But Manco, becoming supreme chief, reunited the tribes under his authority and suppressed their independence. At once the problem changed. To plough, sow, and reap the harvest in a small group was easy. The same activity within the framework of a nation needed real organisation. The outlines of this 'economic' plan appears in a calendar of work drawn up and commented on by Huaman Poma. Everything is foreseen throughout the twelve months of the Inca year.

In January, spin wool.
In February, reclaim virgin land.
In March, protect the fields from plunderers and sparrows.
In April, lead the animals to pasture.
In May, harvest the maize.
In June, harvest the potatoes.
In July, get in the corn and clean the wells.
In August, plough.
In September, sow maize.
In October, repair roofs.
In November, plant green vegetables.
In December, sow potatoes and quinoa.

The critical month was January, when the lack of food added to the menace of cold and damp. To remedy this, Manco set up public granaries, and this was the most popular idea in his system. It must be admitted that Manco did not impose his rule as a chief simply by declaring that he was the son of a god. The people demanded proof, and Manco succeeded because he was able to assure the Indians their food supply and the security they needed. He supplied an answer to their problems.

A religion and a way of life—these two basic foundations of the Inca Empire cannot be separated. If Manco, who was an American, had been asked to explain his plans to a public gathering, he would have said, 'The realm of God can be in this world'. In Huaman's calendar the sacred ceremonies are mingled with the activities in the fields. In November offerings were made to local deities to ensure good rains; at the winter and summer solstices they worshipped the Sun and sacrificed children to him; in September it was the Moon's turn to be honoured. Each of these feasts was an occasion when the peasants gathered together in the principal village, the future capital, Cuzco, or Kasko, 'the navel'.[1] They found there the temple dedicated to the Sun, and the stone houses where Manco and his kindred lived.

It was only a small town—just a few walls. But it was large enough to be divided into two sections: the upper, Hanan, belonged to Manco, and the lower, Hurin, to Ocllo. This separation of man and wife would be incomprehensible were it not that certain Amazon tribes at times applied this custom to their forest clearings; men and women thus sleep together only for the purpose of procreation. The rest of the time the woman is isolated and protected, for on her depends the lineage, and it is she who ensures the precious role of intermediary between the mythical past and the future of the tribe. The separation of Cuzco into two parts was sacred geography. The chroniclers, such as Cobo, were wrong in imagining that two sections had been provided to prevent sedition, or as Montesinos thought, to facilitate counting! The Indians well knew that their capital was a representation in stone of an ancestral tradition.

They visited Cuzco with respect and pleasure. A capital, even if it was only a village, was another world to the Andean peasants, a world outside their usual customs and thoughts. There everything was symmetrical and apart from the land; the sounds, the silence,

---

[1] This was the explanation by Garcilaso de la Vega, and in point of fact, the capital was indeed the centre of the whole life of the Empire. Nevertheless, Father Montesinos thought that Cuzco came from 'Coscoani, coscochanqui', the piling up of the stones needed to level and cover the ground on which the city was built.

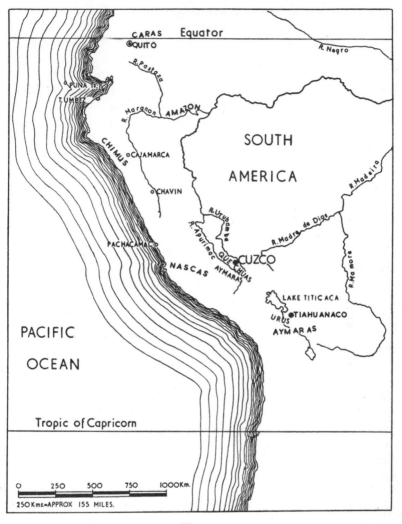

Fig. 21.
At the time of Manco Capac the Empire was limited to the very
small territory immediately around Cuzco, between the two rivers

nature herself, they suddenly found gathered up, assembled on show, ready for consumption. To the country folk, the town always appeared as a turning against nature, and they felt the effects of the restriction. The Indians walked through the streets with caution, slightly ashamed of their sunburn and their big hands. They talked in low voices about the walls that concealed men at work. Wasn't this the house of the potters, moulding vases and jars of clay? And wasn't it here the stonemasons filed the rock down to a fine surface with flints, or pierced holes with bones and damp sand? Was not this hammering the noise made by the metal workers on the plaques of melted gold? Certain of the visitors to the town had brought llama dung to feed the fires under the crucibles. They saw the blowers with their blow-pipes bending over the fusing metal. The crowd of peasants passed round the little secrets of Cuzco by word of mouth.

At last, in the evening, they could relax, drinking, singing, and ogling the girls. This too was part of the capital! And when they had looked and conjectured and touched with the palm to see if it were all true, they departed across the little roads of the plain.

This power of the capital town was Manco's third arm and not by any means the least, since all the essentials of his Empire were assembled there. The members of the citizen tribe formed a new caste, different from and superior to the others. In the system which was growing up, which knew nothing of trade and competition and profit, this caste could only be an official one. From the beginning they had had a distinctive sign of honour—their pierced ears. All the same, the holes were 'half as small again as those in the lobes of the king's ears'. This was a mark of favour with a political meaning, as was everything undertaken by the Incas.

Manco Capac lived a long time—160 years, wrote Huaman Poma with the assurance which characterises poor people for whom the past is a source of wonder.

CHAPTER IV

A SIMPLE WORLD

A portrait of the king–The Inca's territories expand–The basic cell of the Empire–The organisation of work and the division of the popula-tion–Political advantage of the decimal system. The 'quipou', a simple and mysterious apparatus

☐

'LLOQUE YUPANQUI held a lance in his right hand, a shield in his left. His turban was red, his cloak yellow, his tunic purple and ornamented with three finely wrought belts. He wore sandals'. Huaman Poma thus describes the third Inca king in country array.

The name Lloque Yupanqui means 'the left-handed man on whose qualities you may rely'. Our Indian informant seems to in-dicate that he did not have many merits, for he describes him as having a protuberance on his nose, eyes which were too large, and a narrow mouth, and two of his teeth had been broken in a fight. His wife, Cora Ocllo, was of a melancholy frame of mind. She wept without cause, refused the company of her ladies, took no interest in the people, and her only consolation was drink. She neglected her housekeeping and only nibbled raw foods. But the royal couple had many children.

The reason for taking a particular interest in Lloque is not his unhappy domestic life—although this detail helps us to understand the man—but because, according to certain reliable historians, he was the first Inca king to whom has been ascribed a policy of con-quest. His predecessor, Sinchi Roca, the son of Manco, has been left in oblivion in spite of his foreign name [1] and in spite of his son's habit of gouging out his enemies' eyes. Cruelty does not guarantee a place in the heroes' gallery in the edifying story of the Incas! Let us follow the activities of the third king, Lloque. Before begin-ning this account, our loyalty to our informants impels us to give the opinion of Montesinos, the priest who crossed the Andes sixty times. According to him, the existence of the first five Inca kings, of whom Lloque was one, is doubtful. He almost considers them as

[1] Sinchi is a word from the language of the Aymara Indians, meaning chief of a community.

mythical beings.[1] The author's opinion is different, for he agrees with the majority of historians that there were twelve Inca kings, whose names have been preserved to the present day and who were the real founders of the Empire, and who conquered and united the tribes. The fantasy with which popular legend surrounds them does not justify their elimination from the historical world of the Incas. Besides, a story recounted by Huaman Poma would bring conviction of the reality of Lloque, if such were needed. His son, who shared with him the responsibilities of power, was at war with Tocay Capac, or at least with one of the leaders of the mysterious tribe which seems to have resisted the establishment of the Inca Empire. He killed this chief, and from that time the dynasty of Manco held complete domination over the Indian people.

The first preoccupation of a conqueror is to protect his own frontiers. Thus Lloque had a fortress constructed to mark the division between his own country and the territory of his southern neighbours, the Aymaras. This work completed, he hastened to extend the boundaries he had set. He engaged in battles, besieged a town, and his opponents surrendered. 'The son of the Sun pardoned them and recommended that they should be kindly treated'. This historians' phrase sums up the method of pacification used by the Peruvian kings, and they applied it in all the countries which they entered in their role of conquerors. But things went less easily against the Aymaras, for three generations of kings were to struggle to incorporate them into the Empire. It must be recognised that these Indians were not a savage race.

Settled in the province of Colla, in the south, they occupied the whole of the high plateaux and the region round Lake Titicaca. There were amongst them shepherds, farmers and metal workers, making use of the gold, copper, and tin mines. Judging by their descendants, they were equally good warriors, better possibly than the Quechuas from whom the Incas themselves were descended. At least this is the opinion of Garcilaso, who was rather too prone to admire only his own ancestors and too ready to smile at those of others. According to him the Aymaras venerated fountains, streams and rocks and worshipped a sheep, their chief deity. Garcilaso adds, 'These people were in no way civilised. They allowed their daugh-

---

[1] At least this is what he wrote in his *Memorias*. But in *Capaccuna* he records the names of about one hundred Inca kings.

ters to become prostitutes before marriage. In this way vice to them became the greatest virtue, and the most dissolute women were those sought in marriage. The Incas abolished all these practices, but they in no way wished to deprecate the wonderful stories these people told of their origin, for these tales lent support to the origins of the Incas themselves. The king made provision for the government of the country and divided out the remaining lands to bring revenues to the country of the Sun'.

This quotation leads us to enquire what one would think of a historian who wrote, 'Charles VIII, Louis XII, and François I subdued the realms of Naples and Milan and brought the Renaissance to Italy'. Garcilaso made an equally strange error in asserting that the Incas raised the Aymaras from the shadows. Two great scholars, the Frenchman Alcide d'Orbigny and the Englishman Clement Markham, rejected this idea and even went as far as to say that the Quechuas were descended from the Aymaras. This is scarcely probable, but it is certain that the Quechuas and their Inca masters acquired a fair amount of useful knowledge from the Aymaras, if only about the alloy of copper and tin. They also appropriated the word and spirit of a community alliance which was the basis of their economic system, the *aylu*.

Before the assimilation of the Aymaras, although the Inca peoples were in submission to a supreme chief, they remained divided up into a mass of communities whose only link lay in their common kinship (which included their rites and taboos, and, in the long run, their stupidity). The *aylu*, on the contrary, was not only a tribal grouping: the Indians of other clans could share as associate members. The link was no longer blood but the territory where the community worked. The Incas were aware of the gain to be had from this economic association and adopted the principle. All the same, being anxious to preserve the ancient blood heritage, they excluded foreigners from the *aylu*. Thus the true, basic cell of the Empire was formed with the soil as the group link.[1]

Then one day the headmen, who were still the real chiefs of the Peruvian communities, received a visit from an official sent by the

[1] The dynastic kings also followed the system of the *aylus*, but under a slightly different form. Each king, being of divine descent, could at the time of his marriage form a new *aylu* and so separate himself from his ancestral community. According to Sarmiento, at the end of the monarchy there were eleven *aylus* corresponding to eleven kings, plus ten *aylus* descending from the first Incas.

king from Cuzco to explain the new ideas. He was usually the son of a noble family, wearing the cloak and turban. He gave a clear expression of opinion, 'The land belongs to no man, only to God'.

This declaration did not trouble the peasants much, for they possessed no individual patch of ground. But the Inca envoy was always politely asked to explain the practical results which the country folk could expect from this august pronouncement.

'Up to now', said the visitor, 'you have tilled the soil, shared your maize, potatoes, and quinoa, whether the harvests have been good or not. These times are past. Henceforth the land will be divided into pre-determined lots; each head of a family will receive a *tupu*[1] when he marries. On the birth of a son, another *tupu* will be added, and a half *tupu* for a daughter. These lands will not be the perquisite of a single tenant. The Incas' intention is to put the maximum amount of land into cultivation and to vary the crops. You will be helped, for specialists will study the possibility of bringing water to those regions which are without. You will also be provided with manures if llama excrement is insufficient. Finally, during the months when food is scarce, you will receive provisions which will save you from dying of hunger'.

The peasants were unbelieving. How could this be?

'Everything is possible to our father the Sun', replied the envoy, 'for his children occupy lands in the four quarters of our Empire. What some produce others will profit by. You, for example, who have modest herds and are generally satisfied with two llamas to each family, will receive wool from the people of the south without the need of going to war with them, for they are now your fellow-countrymen. But you on your side must work for the Empire. It is very simple: the lands allocated to you are destined for the support of all those, including yourselves, who play their part in ensuring the life of our people. You will cultivate and sow first of all that part of the land which is entrusted to you in the name of the Sun. This will be a pleasure to you, for the harvests are reserved for the worship of the god and the support of the priests during the ceremonial period (the rest of the time they will attend to their own needs, and dig and sow as you do). Then you will move on to the land belonging to soldiers, invalids, the aged, and orphans. Widows can be ignored since our customs oblige their brothers-in-law to care

[1] According to Garcilaso the *tupu* corresponded to a measure of Arabic origin and could be sown with one cwt. of maize.

for them, although if they are war widows they are entitled to special help. Then you will care for your own lands, whose produce is wholly yours. The final portion is divided between your own chiefs and the officials of the Empire. You will see from time to time the *llacta camayoc* or the *suyucoc* who will be charged with

Fig. 22.
*Totrioc
michoc*

overseeing your work and dividing out the harvests. It is also understood that you must work for our king, Apo Capac, son of the Sun. But by his own wish he will be served last and you will not find him any more of a burden than your old communal chiefs of whose former exactions we now rid you. In cultivating the king's lands, maintain a tidy appearance, sing and dance, and at the end, shout "*Hailli*", our cry of victory'.

'*Hailli*', cried the peasants.

'Farewell then', said the envoy and withdrew.

Some years later, a *totrioc michoc* came to inspect the peasant workers, for the state had relaxed its system of control. The *totrioc* was a curious personage, whose ear lobes were split open and hung down on his cheeks. It is known that this was the sign of a celibate prince of the Anqui caste. Unsuitable for military service and for important offices, he was destined from birth for the judicial control of the provinces; he decided local problems and ordered punishments. He ruled with a heavy hand, and it is said that he ordered a peasant to be hung because he had altered the order of work. In this way the people were taught the Inca justice, and any escape from this discipline was impossible. Other envoys of the king appeared, with a counting apparatus, the *quipou,* to make a census of the population ; the chiefs began to fear for their prestige for the *aylus* were divided up like a maize loaf. The growing Empire found that economic problems daily became more complex, and the *aylu* was no longer suitable to ensure regular production. The land was distributed according to the importance of the families, but the peasants displayed a tiresome tendency to consider it their own property. Working as a family encourages a state of mind not always in agreement with the wishes of the state. And so the officials at Cuzco drew up new regulations. Messengers went forth across the valleys and plains to inform the chiefs and explain to them the new rules. By these laws the heads of families *puric* were to assemble in groups of ten; one of them was to be responsible for his section and take the title *chunca camayoc,* meaning chief of ten. His function was to control the share-out of land, to supervise the work, and to ensure the essentials of life to each of his subordinates. On the next level, a *pichca chunca camayoc* controlled five groups, making fifty men in all. Above this grade was the *pachac camayoc,* chief of ten groups, whose duty was to supervise the chiefs of lesser rank, keep daily statistics, and supply information to his superiors, who were charged with the direction of 500, 1,000, and even 10,000 heads of families. *Hupu camayoc,* the chief of ten thousand, was an important person, son of a royal *aylu,* and wearing the golden circles in his ears. Garcilaso, as a half-breed who made no mistakes about the advantages of a military hierarchy, called him general, and the chief of ten he called corporal. This simplicity was suitable for the Inca organisation, which had set up a working army.

These were not the last of the decrees. Still influenced by the decimal system which seemed to penetrate even their political set-up, the Incas arranged for the officials to prepare statistics about the ages of the population. These were divided into ten groups, five of children from birth to the age of sixteen, three of young people from sixteen to twenty-five years of age, and then the group of the *hatunruna* or full-grown men who were compelled to forced labour between the ages of twenty-five and fifty, and finally the last two groups of the old men from fifty to sixty, and over sixty years. According to Cieza de Leon, this was the distribution of population, but once again our friend Huaman Poma insinuates his book of pictures and brings a breath of fresh air to this scene of concentration. According to him, there were indeed ten groups of citizens, whose classification and occupations he gives as follows.

1. AUCA CAMAYOC. The warriors, or more exactly, those who were mobile. The whole male population from twenty-five to fifty.

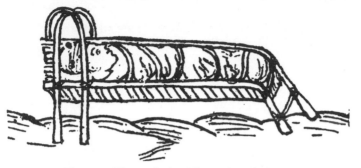

Fig. 23. Uaua Quiro-Picac (see below)

2. PURIC MACHO. From fifty to eighty years. Servants of the noblemen, carrying out light duties.

3. ROCTO MACHO. From eighty to one hundred years and over. 'Old men hard of hearing, only able to eat and sleep, plait ropes and care for the rabbits and ducks'. But they were respected and honoured, mainly because of their sharp tongues.

4. UNCOC RUNA. The sick, deaf, dumb, blind, hunchbacked, dwarfs, and maimed. They gave what service they could and 'were the butts of the rest'.

5. SAYA PAYAC. From eighteen to twenty years. They carried the messages and tended the herds. Practised poverty and abstinence, and had no right to marry.

6. MACTA CONA. From twelve to eighteen years. Tended the herds, hunted birds with a net, and gave the feathers to their chief.

7. TOCILACOC NAMRACONA. From nine to twelve years. They protected the small birds, sown seeds and harvests.

8. PUCLLACOC NAMRACONA. 'Those who play', from five to nine years. Their favourite toy was a spinning top, but it was agreed that they should be 'taught and punished for the good of the realm'.

9. LLULLO VAMRACONA. From early steps to five years. The law permitted parents two years to care for their children, to enjoy them, and 'to save them from falling or being burned'.

10. UAUA QUIRO-PICAC. Infant in cradle.

The women's classification was in line with the men's:

1. AUCA CAMAYOC PA VARMI. The warrior's wife. In between times she wove cloth for garments.

2. PAVACONA. They wove cloth and cooked. Chastity was enforced on widows of a certain age.

3. PUNOC PAYA. They helped to bring up the children if they had the strength.

4. UNCOC CUMO. The cripples. They married other cripples, and dwarfs married dwarfs, blind married blind, and so on.

5. CIPASCONA. Young girls ripe for marriage. These were destined for the temple of the Sun, for the king, for the chiefs and warriors, according to a method of division drawn up by officials of the Empire. 'No one could choose a wife according to his own wishes'. Any infraction of this rule was punished by death. The age limit for marriage was fixed at thirty years.

6. COROTASQUE. 'The little shavelings'. With short skirts and bare feet, they learned to cook, to spin and weave. They prepared the fermented drink, 'chicha'. They were forbidden 'to know woman or man on pain of death'. They were depilated.

7. PAUAU PALLAC. 'The little girls who gathered flowers'. They also helped their parents.

8. PUCLLACOC UARMI NAMRA. 'The little girls who played as they went'. They looked after their little brothers and fetched water for cooking.

9. LLUCAS UARMI UANA. 'Those learning to walk'.

10. CHILLO UAUA UARMI QUIRAUPICAC. As we say, babies. Truly we do not possess the ingenuity of Inca officials.

This persistence in classifying, labelling, limiting, ordering, and in permitting or banning the simplest things of life may be surprising to us. The Indian chroniclers may have freely exaggerated this rigid system when they explained it to the Spaniards. No doubt they thought that to submit men, animals, and lands to an arithmetical law was proof of a very advanced civilisation, as indeed it was for those times. Lloque Yupanqui reigned during that period of our twelfth century when a breeze of spring ran all round the world. In France, Phillipe Auguste suppressed the feudal system and started Bouvines. Besides war, men took a great interest in the compass, the stern rudder, the horseshoe, windmills, and the philosophy of Abélard. Monks built abbeys and drained marshes. The new middlemen discovered the role of intermediary between peasants, workers and nobility, and themselves became rich.

The communal liberties which guaranteed the functioning of commerce were recognised by the king. In this way, whilst Europe embarked on the long road which led to the freedom of the individual, in America progress turned in the opposite direction. Later we shall learn of the maxims of Pachacutec, the ninth king, the thinker of the Inca dynasty, and we shall see that the education and liberty of the people were not the dominating care of the Incas. Rather the impression obtained is that the system which was at first destined to favour agriculture and simplify the administration of the Empire became a means of restraint and at times of oppression. It can well be understood that to settle men on equal terms with a plot of land or a couple of animals, the laws must regulate their spirit as well as their actions!

The task of the first Incas was easy, but easy in the same way as it is simple for children to reorganise their world in their dreams. We cannot but be amazed at the way this system was applied to millions of human beings. The more so since the Peruvians could not write and one wonders how they managed to ensure the working of their system without any papers. How could they record decisions, issue orders, check arms and soldiers, and draw up statistics about the population, list the details of the harvests, record the map of the redivision and exchange of land, not to speak of the daily business of administration? And how could they do this when the Empire was daily expanding and was assimilating new peoples who presented new problems? To this apparently insoluble question the Incas replied with a game of strings. For the *quipou* was nothing but cords and knots and yet was the indispensable instrument of Peruvian life. In the picture of the Inca system, it seems, in appearance, of disconcerting simplicity. But if we place our fingers on it, we are like blind people fingering an object of whose meaning we are ignorant. We need to bring to life the *rune quipoc Inca,* the superintendent of the *quipou,* and let him read us the chapter of the history of his country which he holds in his hands.

At first sight, the instrument appears to be an aid to memory. The Amazon Indians made knots to show how many days they would be absent from their huts, and during their absence their wives unknotted the string. The Incas, starting from this principle, arrived at surprising results, at least as far as the technique was concerned.

Fig. 24. The quipou official

The *quipou,* so simple in appearance, in reality permitted more complex combinations than one would imagine. Erland Nordenskiöld, a specialist in this subject, which he studied at the Musée de l'Homme in Paris, describes the system as follows :

'The *quipou* was composed of a principal greyish-white rope, twisted between two thinner cords. From this rope hung 48 secondary cords, divided into five groups. To some of these cords were affixed extra threads. There were in all 87 cords'. It is known that knots were made on each cord, starting from the lower end—that is to say, the first series of knots represented units, the second tens, and the third hundreds. The small cords were coloured. In collating the accounts given by the chroniclers it may be supposed that the black meant time, red the army or the king, green meant enemies, yellow meant gold, and white meant silver. There were cords of several colours whose position indicated certain meanings. Each *quipou* was arranged to register one of the activities of the administration ; the whole collection recorded the entire life of the Empire. Cobo wrote that there was in fact an apparatus for everything, 'such as tribute, lands, ceremonies, and the different subjects relating to peace and war. Generation after generation, the *quipou camayoc* instructed those destined for this office. The events of the past were explained to them, events recorded in the old *quipous* as well as those they added to the current record. They were thus able to account for everything that had happened in the country since the beginning of the Inca government'. Huaman Poma expresses his opinion even more clearly: 'The whole realm was ruled by the cords'. It is clear that this was no ordinary process of memoranda.

To learn how the Indians used this apparatus we must turn to Father de la Calancha, whose meticulous mind we have already learned to appreciate. He tells us that whatever the subject, a certain sequence of hierarchy was always observed. For example, the first cord was reserved for the lances, the arms of the nobility ; then came the javelins, the arrows and slings. In the population statistics, men of sixty had the right to come first, and then the rest of the population in descending decades. Anxious to explain the technique of the *quipou camayoc,* the monk gives a hypothetical case. ' "Suppose a secretary wished to record the following facts : before Manco Capac there had been no kings, no chiefs, no religion, no worship. The fourth year of his reign, Manco subdued ten provinces, killing many enemies and losing 3,000 of his own men. These victories brought in 1,000 pounds of gold and 30,000 pounds of silver. In gratitude for his success, he proclaimed a feast-day in honour of the Sun". Here was the problem and how could it be solved? The *quipou camayoc* would use a thick black rope to indicate time, and to it he would attach several plain cords with thousands of little knots to indicate emptiness. At the middle of the rope he would fix a red cord by means of a big knot, for', added Calancha, 'the Inca would have been crowned with the red wool turban. In the same way that carmine was the colour of honour for Popes and Cardinals, purple was the insignia of majesty and sovereignty. Four knots would be made in this red cord, meaning the fourth year of the Inca's reign. To the last knot would be attached a brown thread with ten little knots for the ten conquered provinces. To each of these little knots would be fixed a green thread with thousands of new and very tiny knots to indicate the enemies killed in the battle, beginning with the oldest' . . . and so on. The method must now be clear, but the monk, whose fingers must have been very nimble, goes so far as to assert that the *quipou camayoc* made 30,000 knots in a white cord to indicate the 30,000 pounds of silver. This shows that even if he had grasped the principle of the cords, he had not understood how the Incas simplified the decimal system. It seemed clear to him, however, that when the Indians saw their arithmetic lesson they read it quite easily—before the red cord there was nothing; then came Manco Capac, in the fourth year of whose reign took place all that has been recounted.

There is no doubt that even the best-informed of the Inca's subjects would have regarded this account with the greatest bewilderment, for they were infinitely more clever than the monk. Nordenskiöld, who was puzzled by the *quipou* for a very long time, obtained most interesting information about them from the Chaillot Palace. After studying the five groups of cords, he arrived at the following conclusions about the first, second, and fourth groups :

The number indicated by the single cord of the first group was 12.

The number indicated by the nine cords of the second group was 365.

The number indicated by the ten cords of the auxiliary threads of the fourth group was 365.

The total for the five groups was 1,309, and the Norwegian scholar took this to be the solar year, plus 32 months or again 187 weeks. It is plain that in this *quipou,* solar years of 365 days had been calculated. To express the data of Nordenskiöld in its simplest form, the figure of 1,309 was chosen as a starting point, then broken down into solar years and lunar months. So, although it is not known how the Incas arrived at the numbers which are the basis upon which this *quipou* is built, we are faced with a working apparatus whose elaboration necessitated precise astronomical knowledge.

We are now far in advance of the string game which prudent husbands devised for their wives during their periods of absence! In fact, the *quipous* were used by all those in charge of the administration of the country. The high officials at Cuzco—judges, captains, and chiefs of 10,000 families—right down to the simple village headmen had at their disposal instruments whose importance corresponded to the status of the user. They made them themselves as they needed them. So there were quite modest *quipous,* recording the quantities of maize or wool gathered by an *aylu.* There were very complicated ones for the *amautas* who taught the young boys of the royal family, and for the specialists who calculated time. And it may be supposed that the soothsayers recorded their prophecies about certain astronomical data. The line between these two forms of Inca science was not very precisely indicated. It is possible that the *quipous* contained numbers of a magical character. Nordenskiold is of this opinion. He even thinks that *quipous* were buried with the dead to prevent them, by means of magic numbers, from rising from their tombs. It is possible to push the influence of the cords too far. They were buried with secretaries in the same way that arms were placed with the corpses of warriors, and harpoons with those of fishermen, for perhaps they needed them in eternity.

CHAPTER V

BLOOD, BRONZE AND FANTASY

The fourth king subdues the southern provinces–Tiahuanaco–War and diplomacy–Capac Yupanqui reaches the country of the metal workers –The Aymaras teach the Incas to make an alloy of copper and tin

□

EVEN if the Incas could not write they could paint. A priest, Father Cristobal Molina, a companion of the Conquistador Almagro, saw coloured boards in a house at Cuzco on which were painted records of the great events and traditions of the Empire. The viceroy, Toledo, claimed to have examined fabrics which were none other than portraits of the Inca sovereigns and their wives. Another piece of fabric illustrated the creation of the world by Viracocha. These pictures have disappeared, but it is possible that Huaman Poma knew of them and that his legendary drawings of the Peruvian kings were copied from the Inca archives. Thus we turn to him for information about the fourth king in the same way that we did for the first three sovereigns.

Mayta Capac was pale-faced and with fine hands. He was brave and passionate, though at times melancholy. He loved war, and cherished his legitimate wife, since he was both strong and tender. He had many children, a great number of whom died very young. But two of them, Apo Maytac and Bilcac, distinguished themselves in military expeditions to the southward. The chroniclers' accounts often confirm the words of Huaman, and the history of the fourth king comes down to us free from all elements of legend. The period is well established—it was the beginning of our 13th century.

The conquest of the Aymaras, started by Lloque Yupanqui, was to continue in a region far removed from Cuzco, in the neighbourhood of Lake Titicaca. It is not known whether the Peruvians crossed the lake by raft or whether they went round by the western shore, but it is known that they stopped short, with beating hearts, before the strange and magnificent city of Tiahuanaco. No doubt the waters of the lake which in ancient times lapped the walls of the Indian metropolis had already begun to recede,[1] leaving the plain where the Inca troops first appeared. The quays were now ramparts and the town rose up behind this unintentional wall.

The tourist of today who travels in a little train from La Paz to Lake Titicaca stops at a village named Tiahuanaco, as a name board shows. But if he gets out of his carriage to photograph the ruins he will be disappointed. The high plateau stretches bare before him in the blistering sunshine, and apart from the doubtful pleasure of walking in the dust of old broken pottery, there is only the gateway of the Sun through which to pass in his desire to escape. But alas! it opens on to the same plateau! If it were not for the Indian guide who draws attention to certain long stones, the steps of a staircase, or a suspicion of foundations covered with climbing plants, we should refuse to admit that the most ancient city of the Andes had ever existed at this spot. Personal recollections of Tiahuanaco are in fact limited to a few impressions, such as a lamplighter feeling around the four lamps in the village square with his pole; the church built on the ruins of a temple, in which birds were flying about, the only birds in Tiahuanaco; and the curator of this archeological desert. He wore a uniform and was not lacking in manners, for to console us for our disappointment he brought to us at nightfall an old Aymara sorcerer, who told our fortunes with the aid of cocoa leaves and cane alcohol. He called on the Blessed Virgin—Pachamama—the Christian goddess of the land. In his state of ecstasy his wrinkled face relaxed, his eyes shone, and he began to speak the tongue of his ancestors. His head, thrust out of his black blanket, shone with serene happiness. In spite of this, the curator assured us that he foretold death—ours no doubt. I recall Tiahuanaco as a meeting-place for ghosts.

Those Spanish chroniclers who were able to get ahead of their compatriots who were experts at demolishing Indian monuments must have seen a Tiahuanaco that did justice to its noble past. They, like the soldiers of Mayta Capac three centuries earlier, were granted the opportunity for cries of enthusiasm. 'The finest monument', wrote Garcilaso, 'is a man-built hill. The Indians sought to imitate nature, and to prevent the earth from falling in they had strengthened the foundations with masses of well-cemented stones. Elsewhere there were giant monoliths, clad in

[1] Lake Titicaca is today about 15 miles from Tiahuanaco. Its level continues to fall.

long garments and with caps on their heads. There were many very extraordinary buildings, and above all, great doors were made of single stones'.[1]

The writer who seems to have been most astonished by these monoliths was Abbé Diego d'Alcobaca, a friend of Garcilaso. He writes: 'Amongst the buildings at Chuquiyutu, on the shore of the lake, there is a square about 74 square yards in size, and one side of the square is a covered room 45 feet long. The square and the room are one, and have been hewn from the rock. The people of the country believe that these buildings are dedicated to the creator of the universe. Also in this square are many statues of men and women so perfect that they almost seem alive. Some are in the act of drinking, others seem to be preparing to cross a stream, and the women give suck to their babies. The Indians say that these people have been turned to stone for their sins, and above all because they stoned a man who was passing through the district'.

Making allowance for this access of lyric fervour on the part of the Abbé, Tiahuanaco, with its palaces and temples, erected on the bare Andean soil, was worthy of admiration. Although the capture of the city by Mayta's soldiers was the start of Inca expansion, it above all flattered their pride—the pride of an ancient peasant race. Henceforward they went to war as easily as they had hitherto tilled the soil.

The struggle against the Aymaras was harder than had been foreseen. Divided into several groups, they put up a bitter resistance not only to Mayta but to his successors. If it had occurred to them to unite their forces against the Incas, they would perhaps have been victorious. But they did not possess the 'ideal' which lay behind all the actions of the people of Cuzco, and they were defeated, subdued, and colonised. Mayta's campaign, although carried out with troops unaccustomed to war, was a model for all the undertakings of Inca domination. First they had to fight with the tribes situated to the west of the great lake, in the province of Hatun Colla. A peak served as a refuge for the Aymaras, and women and children helped the men to build a fortress there. The Incas decided to reduce it by siege, thus showing a technique which depended not

[1] The most interesting relics from Tiahuanaco have been gathered together at La Paz, Bolivia. There one can see statues of people showing Mongol characteristics, and monolithic stela, which have given birth to the legend of the giant founders of Tiahuanaco. (No one of scientific standing appears to take this legend seriously.)

only on strategy but on a general method of conquest. 'Spare the enemy and his dwellings; soon they will be ours'.[1] Mayta applied this judicious advice of a Peruvian king to his adversaries who were already entrenched in their fortress. He sent them messengers to assure them of his good intentions, simply asking them to submit to the laws and gods of the Empire. In reply, the besieged made a massed sortie, but Mayta avoided a battle, again invested the mountain and renewed his proposals. Once again the reply came in the shape of blocks of stone and arrows. Then the king decided to make the assault, and the fight was short and bloody. The Sun supported the armies of his son—at least this is what the *amauta* professors later taught their pupils in their history lessons. After the battle the Aymara chiefs who had escaped death appeared before Mayta barefoot, with hands bound, and with ropes round their necks. They prostrated themselves and said, 'We deserve death'.

But the king ordered them to stand upright and they were unfettered. The Inca addressed them. 'I have come to teach you and enrich you. Worship our god and carry out our orders for your own good'. He allowed them to touch his knee with their foreheads, which Garcilaso noted as a great favour, recounting this scene with a tear in his eye. But the Inca's forbearance was real, for they never killed unless it was absolutely necessary, showing that they were worthy rulers who themselves had never suffered defeat or slavery. The spirit of vengeance was unknown to them.

Mayta installed his officers in the conquered region to make a census of the inhabitants and their riches. Then he continued his campaign towards the west. The Cordilleras, whose altitude gradually reached fifteen to eighteen thousand feet, imposed a painful journey upon the troops. They camped on snowy plains before crossing thirty leagues of windswept, uninhabited country. It was the road followed by the llama drivers when they brought produce from the valleys to the towns of the high plateaux. But 5,000 soldiers, with arms and provisions, could not so easily scale the mountain paths. When Mayta's troops reached the province of Cuchuna, about sixty miles from the sea, they were exhausted and could not have beaten off any attack. But their reputation had preceded them, and the people of the country, their imaginations dulled by fear, entrenched themselves on a hill. And for fifty days they had time to watch the Inca army, who were patiently await-

[1] Quoted by Sarmiento.

ing their surrender, encamped all around them. Mayta made no attempt to attack the fortress, and at last some men broke out and throwing themselves on the ground, began to eat grass. At last the besieged asked for mercy and came to listen to the king's traditional discourse. Mayta installed a small garrison and some political officers. But he went no farther westwards, for although the sea was only a few days march away, other tribes than the Aymaras occupied the coast, and the Incas did not feel themselves sufficiently strong to undertake their conquest. They returned to the high plateaux.

It is possible that at the beginning of his campaigns, Mayta had no intention of extending his conquest farther south. He had acquired rich lands, immense herds, and the control of the banks of Lake Titicaca as far as the city of Tiahuanaco. He would have been content with this reward, which increased the territory of the Empire by half and strengthened his prestige amongst his neighbours. But the enemies he had defeated were all Aymaras, and he knew that these people and their allies, grouped under the name of Collas, still ruled over other areas to the south of Titicaca. It would be wise to subdue so powerful an enemy before the latter was tempted to reconquer the lost provinces. Mayta launched an expedition to the east of the lake, and in a short time, without opposition, his army again reached the plain of Tiahuanaco. Then he advanced openly towards the south.

The high Bolivian plain lay before the Peruvians—a dry, frozen land, grating under their sandals. A line of mountains enclosed and directed their advance, but their eyes were above all attracted by Illimani, a snowy height of the Andes. Would this giant favour them or protect their enemies? The Incas prayed, as they always did to anything reaching high into the sky. 'Illimani, great chief'. On their left the plain fell away steeply, and at the base of the precipices they could see a waterfall and catch a glimpse of green. But they continued their advance across the plateau, along the immutable route of the migrations of beasts and men. As they marched they raised a dust which stifled them, and when night fell on this high-altitude desert, they threw themselves to the ground, paralysed with cold. Above them the white head of a meteor wrote a message which their leaders interpreted to mean: 'The enemy will be conquered'.

The first big battle took place near the river Huychu. The

Aymaras occupied the right bank and watched the Incas approach
without any sign of fear. They scornfully rejected the king's proposals, and not only that, they waged a terrible and day-long hand-
to-hand fight. The Aymaras had no knowledge of the science of
open warfare and fell upon their adversaries, either killing or being
killed. They had formidable arms, bronze clubs with which they
broke more than 500 Inca skulls, but this was insignificant compared with their own losses of 6,000 dead. When dawn broke the
next day they realised their defeat, for the Inca army had surrounded them and, only a sling's throw away, were awaiting, in
battle array, the first ray of the sun as a signal for attack. The
moment of extermination had come when the king appeared in
his litter, and calming the eagerness of his soldiers he once again
sent messengers to offer peace to the enemy. The Colla chiefs, red
with the blood from their wounds, approached the Inca king and
knelt before him. The interest of the conquerors was soon attracted
to the arms and many other bronze objects the Aymaras placed at
their feet. The Incas were skilled workers in gold and copper, but
they knew nothing of other metals, or at any rate could not com-
bine them. They had been intrigued by the few tools they had collected in the region of Tiahuanaco, and now they were in the very
heart of the country whose people possessed the secret of the fusion
of metals. There now appeared before the Peruvians' eyes a more
coveted wealth than the thousands of llamas requisitioned during
the campaign. In the limpid night air of the high plain they saw a
line of red fires; these were the smelting furnaces set up on the
heights around Potosi. But Mayta did not take possession of the
mining centres of the Aymaras, for his return route was not secure.
The king preferred to organise the conquered country and leave to
his sons the task of penetrating farther south. Two captains, Bilcac
and Apo Maytac, and above all Capac Yupanqui, the heir to the
throne, completed their father's undertaking.

Huaman Poma writes this simple phrase under the portrait of
Capac Yupanqui: 'He reigned over the Quechua and Aymara provinces'. He was the fifth sovereign of the dynasty, and he united
two great peoples under a common destiny. He had the reputation
of a clever man, familiar with occult sciences and able to converse
with spirits. It is said that his wife had nervous attacks, when she
bit and scratched the ladies of her suite. This did not prevent Capac

Yupanqui from being a great prince, for he changed his wife and continued to ask the advice of the gods in the conduct of affairs of state. The army he collected for his expeditions was the largest and the best disciplined the Peruvians had ever had. He led this army without opposition as far as the point reached by Mayta, to the banks of Lake Popo. To the east the neighbouring country was cut into valleys and deep ravines opened before him. Just as the king was preparing for a difficult campaign, the headmen asked for an audience.

They said that the two powerful chiefs of the province were constantly at war; they were unable to settle their differences by other means, and the whole region was threatened with total destruction. Their names were Cari[1] and Capana, and they wanted the king to arbitrate. A way of peaceful conquest was thus offered to Capac Yupanqui, and he called together the two opponents. Face to face, he begged them to state their claims and had officials note their replies on a *quipou*. Then he counselled them wisely: 'You are powerful chiefs, and you spend your time destroying all that your vassals produce. Your ancestors have left you a heritage which you are ruining. Take care lest other chiefs profit by your disagreements, invade your lands and drive you out'. Nearly 10,000 Peruvian soldiers surrounded the meeting-place, and the Inca's words had a meaning which the complainants could not disregard. They declared that they would henceforth live in harmony. 'You must accept the laws of the Empire', concluded the king. 'The Sun assures peace and prosperity to all his children'. Then he gave them vicuña wool garments, some jewels set in gold, and an armed escort so that they could return in peace to their homes. Without having thrown a single missile from his slings, Capac Yupanqui extended his realm to the outskirts of the virgin forest to the east and to the Potosi mines in the south.

Garcilaso describes Potosi in the following terms: 'A sugar-loaf hill rose from the plain, one league in circumference at the base and nearly a mile high. The crest was rounded, and at times in the morning, covered with snow'. In fact the whole region is laid waste by wind and cold, and were it not that the earth contains a quantity of minerals, man would not think of living there. But this is one of the extremities of the metal road across the continent—that

[1] The word 'cari' is found again amongst tribes of Caribbean and Arawak origin, and is a term used in connection with the fusion of gold and copper, particularly in Guiana. (Recorded by P. Rivet.)

strange trade route which links the north of Chile with Guiana. The Spanish chroniclers have written so fully about the treasures discovered by the Conquistadors that we are fully informed about the metallurgic activities of the Indians. But it is an ethnological scholar, Dr. Rivet, whom we invite to accompany us in this the most astonishing discovery of the American world.

He writes: 'The story of El Dorado, which exercised so many minds during several centuries, which attracted so many and foolish undertakings, caused so many disasters and so much human sacrifice, came to life one day because, in a lost corner of Guiana, an obscure Carib or Arawak craftsman discovered that by combining the native gold with copper, an alloy could be produced which was slightly oxidised, and when polished acquired a singular lustre'. This technique, extolled by a number of travellers, including the great adventurer Raleigh, places, as clearly as a name on a map, the origin of the most advanced gold industry of the continent. Thanks to this, the Colombian goldsmiths quickly brought it to perfection and could gild or silver metals, weld them, and give them a patina which preserved them. The Chibcha Indians spread this method as far as the Equator, and from there, at an earlier period than that of the Incas, it reached the Peruvian coast. The people of the high plateaux of Peru and Bolivia only learned it later, at the time of their territorial expansion. Throughout this region of the Andes, the Indians worked gold and copper separately, or, as in the case of the Aymaras, they made an alloy of copper and tin.[1] Lead was also used in their metal work, but only after long and fruitless research. Garcilaso tells us how the properties of lead were discovered in the region of Potosi. 'At first the Indians encountered many difficulties in melting silver because it would not soften but burned away. But greed and the need for arms were so strong that they found the remedy, which was lead, a metal of poor quality but which was plentiful at Potosi. Mixed with silver, it became solvent, and because of this the Incas called it *Curuchec,* which means that which causes something to melt'.

The Peruvians were very ready to realise the advantages to be gained from Bolivian minerals and the knowledge of alloys, especially as their type of civilisation required tools as well as ornaments. Bronze axes, chisels and trepans assured the glory of the Inca Empire, but it was the gold pendants and statuettes which precipitated

[1] Cassiterite (lead oxide), easily melted and rich in metal.

their downfall because they aroused the greed of the Spaniards. As the centuries roll back, the connection between the Indians' implements and their destiny as a people conforms to worldly logic. If we climb the South American metal trade route we observe first of all that the most advanced civilisations are settled in the neighbourhood of the metal lodes of the Cordilleras. Next we discover that the Incas, the best organised of the Indian Empires, possessed the most extensive range of metallurgical knowledge, based on gold, copper, silver, lead, and tin. Their northern neighbours, and especially the Caras on the Equator, were influenced by them and also by the Colombians; they formed a sort of neutral belt between the Incas and the Chibchas. These latter were supreme amongst the workers in gold, but they knew nothing of the 'heavy' metal industry of the Peruvians, which was perhaps useless to them for their particular conception of life. Then at the end of the chain there were the tribes of the upper Orinoco and of Guiana, the kinsmen of the continental peoples, but remaining faithful to the virgin forest. Many of the early explorers met these Indians, naked, but proud of their gold ornaments, the *curicuris,* which dilated their nostrils or dragged down the lobes of their ears. Amongst them must be sought the first appearance of gold in South America— perhaps even in America itself.

The Indians of North America treated gold and silver only by a primitive method of hammering them when cold or hot. The Mexicans of the fourth century had no metal industry. The Mayas of the first Empire knew nothing of copper, and those of the new Empire in the 10th century were ignorant of bronze. The South American Indians had outstripped them in the science of metals; it is even possible that it was they who brought this knowledge to Florida, across the sea from the Antilles, and to Mexico by way of the Pacific Ocean. One remembers the raft met with by the pilot Bartholomew Ruiz some leagues from the Gulf of Guayaquil, before the Conquistadors came to Peru. We know the complete list of articles on the raft; amongst the gold and silver objects there were crowns, belts, bracelets, leg ornaments, hair tweezers, bells, necklaces, mirrors and cups. Where were these Peruvian goods going, if not to Mexico? Were they not following the trade route, of which there were still many traces? It might perhaps be objected that these commercial links are very recent, for the 15th century was but yesterday. But what can be said about the two gold discs found in Guatemala by the American scholar Lothrop, which bore the motifs of the ancient Chavin civilisation? Were the Peruvian Indians already visiting the other American peoples centuries before the Christian era?

Capac Yupanqui's soldiers, who are chronologically nearer to us than the Chavin epoch, could not have answered this question. At Potosi and in the mining centres of their new allies, the Aymaras, they simply admired the nightly spectacle of the metal-smelting furnaces. The flames leapt up from the furnaces, or *huaira*, placed near the summit. Cobo writes; 'There were so many of them that the mountain was illuminated'. The wind round the heights fanned the hearth, which men fed with dry shrubs or llama excrement.

*Fig. 25.
Huaira, or
metal-smelting
furnace*

The furnace itself was of baked earth, with thick walls pierced with holes to let in the air. It was filled with a mineral which had been laboriously crushed with an enormous block of hard granite. Four Indians were scarcely sufficient to move the crusher, the *maray*, on the slab. Each apparatus and each furnace produced a minute quantity of metal, but the work never stopped, and from the open holes in the ground where the mineral was mined, to the workshops where the metal was refined in a series of smelting furnaces, thousands of Indians toiled to and fro, day and night. For the greedy Incas this must have been a heartening sight.

CHAPTER VI

THE NASCA INTERLUDE

Expedition towards the Pacific Ocean–The necropolis civilisation–The pleasant decadence of the Nasca tribes

☐

DURING his reign Capac Yupanqui absorbed into the Empire not only the Aymaras but also the Lucana tribe, who lived four or five days' march to the west of the Apurimac river. He had then reached a warm region, but the hills and plains which still divided it from the sea were occupied by people whom the king did not seek to conquer. He learned of their customs, and two of these, although of very different kinds, showed a certain degree of evolution; these were homosexuality and the irrigation of arid lands. The Incas were familiar with irrigation systems, but much less so with sodomy. Capac Yupanqui then appointed one of his sons, Captain Auqui Topa, to subdue these interesting neighbours. He had confidence in Topa, for as a mark of homage he had several times brought his father the severed head of an enemy. According to Huaman Poma, always up to date in historical details, he also cut off his enemy's essential parts.

The expedition was more of a military journey than a war. The enemy carried fantasy to the point of dancing in front of the rude peasants who had come down from the heights to conquer them. Had the Incas forgotten that in former times the coastal Indians and the people of the high plateaux had many trade relations with each other? The Incas had forgotten nothing, but the Chavin and Tiahuanaco epochs had disappeared into the past; now Cuzco was the only metropolis. The river dwellers near the Pacific Ocean did not immediately realise the importance of this change. Bathed in tropical heat, they had passed several centuries in peaceful decadence. They cultivated the land near the rivers and along the old canals, or they relaxed in the small isolated towns, imitating the weaving and pottery which had been the glory of their ancestors. The Incas were scornful of the indolence they showed under all circumstances. Captain Topa, although he admired the rich valley

6. Chimu Culture: vase.

[*Musée de l'Homme, Paris*]

7. Fortified temple: Tantamaya region.
(Pre-Inca Culture of the Upper Marañón.)
[*Agence Internationale*]

The ancient Festival of the Sun is still performed today
at the Inca fortress of Sacsahuaman, near Cuzco.

of Hacari as he passed through it, ate fresh fish, and burned a few inverts, was, on the whole, disappointed with his expedition, and his soldiers even more so. To these mountaineers the Pacific Ocean meant only a dangerous frontier, a territory accessible to spirits. Perhaps, quite simply, they did not care for sea-bathing.

The Peruvian soldiers were very little interested in things or in

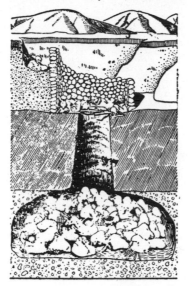

Fig. 26.
Paraca
burial
chamber

the peoples whom they had not killed or vanquished. They were true warriors; save for death or plunder, their world was empty. The truly remarkable spoils which they might have brought back from the Nasca country escaped them completely. There should have been scholars accompanying the troops. But Yupanqui's son was not Bonaparte, and he found in his army no Captain Bouchard who was sufficiently learned to discover a wonderful stone like that at Rosetta, in the Nile delta, nor had he a Champollion capable of deciphering it. The Incas attached little importance to the civilisation which had, in the past, made this region one of the most advanced in America. The silence of the chroniclers on this subject is typical, which is a great pity. Without the goodwill of investigators such as Julio Tello, we should be as ignorant as they were.

The story begins with the Chavin epoch, the centuries during which Indian thought was obsessed with the presence of the gods. The jaguars of the virgin forest, deified in the temple of the

Cordillera, had come down the roads from the eastern side as far as the Pacific coast. Or at least their image did, inscribed on pottery, cloth or stone. Priests came also to explain the religion. They advanced towards the south by stages, alongside the sea, and finally settled on the Paraca peninsula, where hills, now bare, surround a bay of calm water—a suitable place to settle a fishing people.

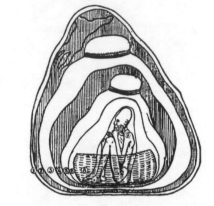

Fig. 27.
Paraca
method
of
burial

Nothing of the settlement can now be seen, unfortunately, but the place has become an immense burial ground. Indeed, archeologists who wish to define the Paraca civilisation by a key-word are obliged to speak of a civilisation of tombs. The earliest settlement, according to them, corresponds to a race of cave-dwellers, and the later one to a necropolitic culture. The earlier tombs contain about 50 bodies, the later ones 400 or more. The burial rooms were hewn out of red porphyry, 18 feet under the surface.

The skeletons of the cave era were badly protected from the weather, but their skulls, which had been deformed or trepanned, reveal that their owners had a notable aesthetic sense and also a knowledge of magic. During the later period, the more recently buried corpses are in a very good state of preservation, as they had been embalmed. Their skin is dark, and sometimes black, but the face is painted red. It is difficult to establish actual contact with the body, for it has been swathed with meticulous care in more than 60 yards of cloth. There are not only strips to keep the body rigid, but actual compartments whose appearance resembles the funerary urns of certain regions in the Andes. It is the inviolate world of eternity as conceived by the men of Paraca.

The dead man is at the bottom of the chamber, naked, and seated in a basket. Clothes have been placed within the inner envelope: cloaks, tunics, shirts (*unkus*), sandals, all in such numbers that one can realise with what care the relatives of the dead man made preparations for his last journey. Perhaps he would need them all, as well as the roots of manioc or grains of corn which had been placed

Fig. 28. Paraca pottery

within his reach. All the peoples of the world have tried to simplify the mystery of death, whether they are the proud ones who reserve their places in the crematorium ovens, or the timid ones who arrange to have themselves embalmed. The materialistic Paraca Indians took all precautions. In the funerary chamber they buried with the dead man all that appertained to his position and fame, as well as the sacred riddles which it was thought would become familiar to him in the silence. Did not Dr. Tello's fingers tremble when he unearthed these objects from this well-regulated world, and without which the deceased would have been only a heap of bones? We explorers all desecrate graves, but perhaps we may be forgiven simply because we have discovered some secrets of the men of olden times, or have catalogued, as at Paraca, the 99 objects contained in a single burial chamber. Here is the list:—

    22 shrouds
     1 stone club
    37 slings of aloe fibre
     2 feather fans
    23 gold dishes, packets containing powder for dying, shell bracelets, pieces of tanned leather, and
     1 wig made of human hair!

There was also pottery. The artisans of the first period liked to imitate the wooden containers of their ancestors. Cups and vases were painted green, yellow and red, and ornamented with Chavin motifs or the geometrical lines inspired by another Andean civilisation, that of the Huaydos. (The two upper rows in the illustration.) The ceramics of the period of the occupants of the necropolis were

Fig. 29.
Nasca
decoration

finer, rather austere, and often reproduced natural objects, especially tropical fruits (as seen in the bottom row of the illustration).

The story of the Paraca people, which began at the time when the priests from the Cordilleras reached the shores of the Pacific, does not come to an abrupt end in the tombs. The Paracas softened the cruel Chavin civilisation and deprived the sacred animals of their menacing crocodiles. Then they built up a peaceful form of existence which tended to free them from religious fears and directed their attention to human affairs. They were skilled surgeons, working with obsidian knives and closing trepanned skulls with gold plates. They were clever craftsmen, working with a variety of techniques, and making the gold plates for trepanning. And there were artists and poets, for their skill in ornamenting their clothing is indeed poetic. You would expect five or six colours on a simple turban, but they would use ten, and the colours are as fresh today as 2,000 years ago. This variety of experiment with dyes, and indeed the whole skill of the textile workers, permitted their artists to depict their world in all its nuances. Some saw it as a world within themselves, shot through with a kind of radiation of things; others cleverly copied from nature. But the majority remained obsessed with the mystery of creation and endeavoured to reproduce in a single creature all the forms of which it was composed. But to some artists, man and man alone was the greatest thing in the universe, and they were the first laymen of the continent. It came about as follows.

The Nascas, settled farther south, reached an equal stage of perfection in the decoration of their pottery. The original inspiration

Fig. 30.
Nasca
decoration

was the same, as the Chavin priests pursued their way southward. One finds the chimera with a feline head, a reptile's body, and four paws greedily beating the air. Its tongue snatches at the fruits of the earth and at men, and it is accompanied by lightning. But the primordial hunger seems sated, and the power of the gods becomes more secret. Snakes intertwined, parrots, owls, and frogs appear as symbols. Then man, with a puma's mask, risks hunting at nightfall, under the protection of the moon, and with his head covered with snakes. Then he appears crossing the sky, as if he were not

Fig. 31.
Nasca
decoration

quite sure of his powers as a man, and clasping his weapons in his hands. Finally he is free and self-confident, no longer a miserable head-trophy in the claws of a god. But it is the head, the seat of the spirit, that still remains the most important charge. From birth, the skulls of Nasca babies were placed between two boards to direct their growth towards the heavens and to make them take the shape of a crown, and in this way to be superior to all other living people.

To the Indians, deforming a man's skull was evidently a gesture of independence, for they themselves changed the natural order of things.

These people knew how to laugh; they loved to play. They had held rackets and balls in their hands. They were civilised. How far

Fig. 32. Haidas decoration

did they spread? Were they navigators? Did the raft met by the pilot Bartholomew Ruiz contain the products of their craftmanship amongst the rich materials they carried? The mystery which surrounds the peoples of the south coast of Peru will not last for ever. Could not the marine monster which the Haidas[1] Indians imagined be the cousin of the gods of Chavin and Paraca?

One day, thanks to the patient work of scholars, the American Indians will be able to find again their great kinship in the tribes which have wandered for centuries across the continent. Will they recognise one another? Or will they think, as the Incas thought when faced with the decadent Nasca tribes, that it is too late?

---

[1] It must equally be noted that similarities between the Haidas and the people of Oceania have been found. The possibility of Oceanic influence on the peoples of the south coast of Peru cannot be ruled out. (For example, the gourds found in the Paraca tombs.) The Nascas present an important field for study of the relations between Oceania and America.

CHAPTER VII

THROUGH THE PARROT, THE INCAS ACQUIRE THE FOURTH WONDER OF THE WORLD

Prince Roca learns to chew coca–He becomes king and decides to conquer the territories to the east–The adventures of Captain Tiger– The Empire of the four provinces is administered by men who are living dossiers–Political philosophy

□

CUZCO gave a great welcome to Captain Auqui Topa as he entered the town, standing in his palanquin, borne by four of his soldiers. Drums, trumpets, and the victory cries of the citizens accompanied him to the house of the king. The people feasted for several days and learned from the soldiers the curious story of the Nasca country.

Capac Yupanqui, hearing of the peaceable nature of the inhabitants, decided to send his eldest son, heir to the throne, to extend his domination along the sea-coast. This would be a good way of inuring him to war without his running too many risks. He was a tall, smiling fellow named Roca, the image of his mother, who was Yupanqui's second legitimate wife. He was well-spoken; his professors thought well of him, as did the young ladies. His father informed him of his intention and entrusted to him the command of all his troops. 'You will take with you', he said, 'several Nasca families, destined for settlement in the temperate valleys of the river Apurimac. There is no doubt that the Nascas, supported by the laws of the Empire, will become good husbandmen'. Roca bowed to his father, hoisted his colours of bright green and deep blue, and set off on the road to the coast.

When he returned, after travelling eighty leagues southward by the seashore and receiving the surrender of the inhabitants of this region, the king was happy to see him again. He thought his son looked well, but he was troubled when he saw that Roca was putting the little green leaves of the coca in his mouth and chewing them constantly. He asked if Roca had acquired this habit during his expedition. Roca admitted this and handed to his august father an elegant woollen bag filled with coca leaves. But the king would not chew it. The prince explained that the people on the slopes of the valleys cultivated these small trees, whose leaves had the property of dulling hunger and cheering the spirits of those who chewed it. But it was best to make the coca more palatable by adding a little burned earth or quinoa ash. The effect was immediate and harmless.[1] The king sighed and told his son that he already knew about coca and had experimented with it. 'Peoples in warm countries cultivate this small tree', he said, 'but its use is not as harmless as you think. In any case do not recommend it to the people'. Prince Roca continued to masticate his leaves, thinking of the ten thousand soldiers in his army who were doing the same thing at that very moment. To bring back the smile to his father's face he showed him a sort of white flour. 'What is this?' asked the king. 'Bird excrement',[2] replied the prince. Yupanqui was very interested in this product when his son assured him that it was a fertile manure. The people on the coast were very satisfied with it. 'Here is something more useful to our people than coca', said the king.

Yupanqui died soon after, certain that Roca was worthy to succeed him. In fact, after the two years of mourning had passed, the sixth sovereign undertook the conquest of the Chancas, his northern neighbours. With 20,000 men and four generals, he quickly accomplished this, but met with resistance from the sons of the Puma. They were the more unwilling to submit because they had once held sway over the Quechua tribes. They were humiliated when they saw the Quechuas coming to conquer them, and they swore that they would one day take their revenge. Roca installed his officers in the country and returned to Cuzco.

The Empire had now assumed the proportions of a great state. It comprised the Bolivian plateaux, the Cordilleras from Lake Titicaca on the south as far as the banks of the river Mandaro on the north, and was open to the Pacific Ocean for more than 300 miles. Its lands were favourable for a varied agriculture and the raising of llamas, and the soil was rich in minerals. A logical or even an ambitious spirit should have been satisfied. But some demon of

---

[1] Coca (*Erythroxylon coca*) yields cocaine when the leaves are treated with ether. The mastication of coca is always accompanied by the absorption of alkaline substances in such a way as to isolate the alkalis contained in the leaves. Even today the Indians of the Cordilleras remain faithful to this practice, and its noxious effect is obvious.

[2] Guano.

adventure troubled Roca's sleep. Towards the rising sun the frontier was not well defined, for there lay the virgin forest. The Indians of the Cordilleras did not need to make any great effort of memory to recall the endless travels of their ancestors, but the present situation of the Empire effaced past misfortunes. They were no longer poor devils of emigrants wandering in the marshes; they were Incas. Roca desired crocodiles, parrots, and monkeys to enliven his gardens. It remained only to go and find them.

This task was allotted to Captain Apo Camac, surnamed Otorongo (the Tiger). Although he had only ten thousand men to accompany him, the expedition took on the appearance of a military campaign, because Captain Tiger was the first Inca explorer of the Amazon. He showed a real understanding of native affairs; he married a girl from the woods who chewed manioc pulp for him and offered it to him, night and morning, mixed with water. But before Captain Tiger attained these delicate pleasures which were the reward of greed and love, he was obliged to undergo all the sufferings of a simple explorer in the virgin forest. Of course, the first stages were not too difficult; the party travelled down the length of the river Paucartambo, and apart from the vertigo experienced when looking down at it from the summits, the obstacles were the same as were met with anywhere in this district of transition between the Andes and the forest. But as soon as he had to hack his way through the tropical vegetation his troubles began. And these have always been the same for thousands of years—humidity, lack of food, mosquitos, and the disagreeable impression that the vegetable world is never-ending. There were plenty of parrots, but they were not yet tame and not numerous enough to appease the hunger of ten thousand soldiers. The men ate wild fruits and then roots; history does not say if they ate those of their number who died, but it is likely. Nothing is more pitiful than the condition of thousands of men wandering in the dim light of the virgin forest and jostling around like a herd of blind cattle. Captain Tiger saw that his expedition was claiming more victims than a battle on the Cordilleras, but he continued his advance.

The reward of his efforts was a forest clearing, shining in the sun. This was not very much, but it was life regained! Those who have thrust aside the last creepers which separated them from an Indian forest clearing have experienced the same profound joy. The noise of men at work, the laughs, or simply the waiting silence, everything catches hold of us with a kindly hand and draws us forward towards the light. Whatever the reason which has led the traveller to the clearing, at this moment he becomes a prodigal son welcomed by his own people. Apo Camac, the Tiger, came to conquer, but faced with the forest Indians he laid down his arms. The survivors of his expedition approached and sat by the hearths, so weary and at the same time so happy that the 'savages' shared their food with them and smiled at them.

Only the surname of these tribes survives—the Chunchos. With a hesitant finger, like the Jivaros and Iawas of today, they touched the soldiers' clothes and skin. They should have been able to recognise themselves amongst them, for they sprang from common ancestors. But the Incas were already men of another world. When their strength returned, so did the memory of their city, their fields, their masters. Nothing enslaves like slavery! They tried to explain the rules of the life of which they were so proud. This was not difficult, for the forest Indians not only had the gift of understanding their neighbours' dialect, but they could even more easily read their thoughts. The Tiger spoke of the king and the Sun god during his conferences with the chiefs he had gathered together. The men of the woods listened in silence. But as days and nights succeeded other days and nights, time, whose hours were only measured by the fires of dawn or the fluting of Pan pipes at dusk, was forgotten. Apo Camac wearied of repeating his political message and gave orders that the animals required by the king should be caught alive. When he considered that the numbers of parrots, monkeys, and baby jaguars were sufficient, he assembled his men and ordered them to set out on the homeward road. The tracks they had left on the outward journey would guide them to the Cordilleras, but his own decision was made—he would stay with the Chunchos. There were murmurs from his troops, but Captain Tiger had made his choice between the triumphal reception at Cuzco and the peace of the forest clearings. When the last of his soldiers had disappeared into the forest, he slowly turned his steps towards the hammock where his plump naked wife awaited him.

The king was very annoyed at the attitude of Apo Camac, but the forest animals which the soldiers had brought back in cages calmed his displeasure, and these were now ready to enliven the gardens of his new palace. Along the whole of one side of the central square was an austere façade built from grey stones perfectly

Fig. 33. Marriage amongst the Antes Indians

placed in spite of their diversity of shape.[1] The roof was of rushes and the windows were limited to a few openings. Nothing could have led the citizens of Cuzco to suppose that this great house was in any way luxurious. But inside the palace, where only the priests, the high officials, and the king's intimates were admitted, the dynasty's opulence was freely in evidence. The wall facings were painted in vivid colours, and the patio was decorated with statues of gold. There was no particular elegance—the furniture was limited to stools for conversation, wooden platforms on which to sleep, and silver mirrors for the king's toilet. It must be admitted that Roca had the good taste to lay down Nasca rugs, the softness of which was agreeable to his feet. The animals added an exotic note to this estate, where the most precious products of the Empire were assembled.

The parrots served not only to amuse the children; they also reminded Roca that his authority now extended over the virgin forest. Each day and each moment the Incas were reminded of the expansion of their Empire simply by glancing at the capital city. Cuzco had become the meeting-place of the caravans transporting grain or minerals, of captains on leave, of chiefs on a visit. At the same time the city had developed in no haphazard way but according to a plan which made Cuzco a faithful reproduction of the Empire. Its inhabitants and almost all its officials were assembled according to a geographical plan. Those responsible for the northern province lived in the north of the capital; those responsible for the south lived in the south, and so on. This dividing out has a touching simplicity about it, but it was possible to foresee the spirit of conquest of the regime because the situation of future associates of the Empire was reserved beforehand. By assigning the eastern sector of Cuzco to the new administration for the virgin forests, the king assured to himself the control of the four cardinal points. And on that day the Inca Empire assumed its true name—Tawantinsuyu, the Four Quarters of the World. A compass card with the four points is sufficient to express in concrete form the administrative division of the Empire.

A member of the royal family was placed at the head of each province, and the four viceroys formed the Grand Council of the Apocuna—or at least the permanent nucleus of this Council. All the information about the Empire's activities converged on this

[1] This house had an over-all measurement of 300 feet square.

body. From the humble chief of ten families to the Apocuna, the chain of controllers, general supervisors, regional chiefs, and the officials of the *quipou* established a permanent contact. Nothing escaped the central organisation, which, since it was in possession of all economic and political information about the provinces, could

Northern Province
(Chinchasuyu)

Western Province   Eastern Province
(Contisuyu)   (Antisuyu)

Southern Province
(Collasuyu)

Fig. 34. The four quarters of the Inca World

compare them and take decisions affecting the interests of all. The thousands of officers at Cuzco were always in a position to supply the Council with all the details it required, and which they had recorded on their cord apparatus. These men were able to give statistics of population, of promotion, about stores, men in prison, the state of productivity, and about Dallos, the superman—they were in fact living dossiers! These files were kept up to date and were at the disposition of a small number of trained brains. In this Empire, which in the end absorbed more than twenty million subjects, the number whose task it was to do the thinking for the rest could be counted on the fingers.

In the course of the three or four centuries of the Inca Empire, the policy of conquest never let up and the administrative machine was never enlarged. Was this a perfect system? It was so inasmuch as it eliminated risks, limited the margin of chance, prepared for the future, and above all reduced man to the role of a perfect operative. In this aspect the Inca system had a modern appearance. Just as today, when the policies of the world are orientated by a dozen scholars and scientists, the policies of the Incas were decided by a few people with big ears who reserved to themselves the domain of knowledge. But since it was made up of members of the royal family, how was it that this *élite* did not become exhausted? A phrase attributed to Roca gives the answer.[1] 'Knowledge must be acquired by the nobility and the nobility alone, otherwise the people would become proud. Their pride would prejudice the state'.

The king's words were not the expression of a wish. He had built, beside his palace, the first college in the capital, the *Yacha huasi*, reserved for the children of the ruling caste. The princes, and later the sons of the nobility, were compelled to go to school (the princesses, *Nustas*, never went, as learning was useless to women). For four years, young people, chosen by the king by reason of their birth, and under the direction of the Amautas, the wise men of Inca blood, learned history, tradition, religion and poetry, as well as the use of the *quipou*. At the same time they indulged in sports, running especially, as this was one of the tests undergone at the ceremony of initiation to puberty. They had to compete in a cross country run of about nine miles, and the winners received short breeches decorated with feathers, and found themselves entrusted with the responsibility of looking after their fellows. They were already marked out as future chiefs. On leaving the college they were ready for all the duties with which the king might entrust them. As for the children of the people, Roca limited their education quite simply. 'They must', he said, 'follow their father's trade'.

[1] Quoted by Garcilaso de la Vega, from Father Blas Valera.

CHAPTER VIII

SUFFERING, DEATH AND MEDICINE

The king 'with tears of blood' visits his subjects and honours his shrines–Different ways of hunting demons–The confessional as a curative measure–Peruvian medicine–Trepanning

☐

THE king ordered his palanquin to be lowered to the ground, and immediately the palm bearers who accompanied the procession swept the ground which the Inca's feet would touch. Around them was the sullen afternoon of the Cordilleras. Grey clouds covered the sky from one summit to another, and across the plain stretched the monotonous chequer board of fields despoiled of their harvest. Set in the farm-land, the sparrow scarers resembled orderly ranks rather than a welcoming crowd. A little house with a thatched roof stood by the side of the road, and near it a peasant, bent double, trembled and recited prayers. The king asked him to show him his dwelling, but the man's emotion was so great that he was incapable of moving a step, and the sovereign approached the door alone. A murmur went up from a group of officials and soldiers who accompanied him. Did the king really wish to enter this miserable hut? The king wished it so. He bent down, protecting the three red plumes in his hair with his hand, and crossed the threshold. In the half-light he struck his nose against a strip of dried meat, then, becoming accustomed to the poor light, he looked around him. He made out the working tools: a big spade and a fork placed against the wall. On the ground embers flickered amongst some gnarled branches. A *coui* (an Indian pig) trotted between his legs, and in reply to the little cries uttered by the animal came the whimper of a baby. He then saw a whole family huddled together in the darkest corner of the hut—an old man, a woman, and some youngsters, a collection of terrified faces. Only the crying baby, dragging itself across the damp earth, came towards him. The mother, to avoid an act of sacrilege, glided to her child and lay down over him. 'It is time to give him milk', said the Inca quite simply. The woman raised herself on all fours, with her breasts hanging so that the child

Fig. 35. The king and queen in their palanquin

8. Carved stone head of a man.
(Pre-Inca Culture of the Upper Marañón.)

[*Agence Internationale*]

9. Garo, the one-time capital
of Yaro Vilca, where the
Indian Huaman Poma
was undoubtedly born.

[*Agence Internationale*]

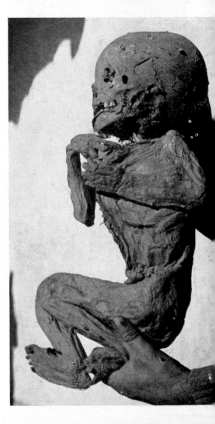

Mummy from pre-Inca ruins.

[*Agence Internationale*]

could suck in the traditional way. The king asked if there were not some spot where the child could be settled on some coverings to play as children should. But no one dared to reply. The silence was broken by the panting breaths of the old man. *Zamaipiti,* pneumonia, thought the king, and turned to leave the hut. Outside, the members of his suite bowed as he passed. He walked slowly towards his palanquin and was annoyed to see the queen, the slender Ipauacoma, pulling the tongue of her tame parrot. He seated himself facing her, and as he was borne away, soothed by the easy pace of the porters, he turned a last look on the little hut. The peasant had not moved and was still trembling.

In this way, Yahuar Huacac, the seventh ruler, visited his Empire, learning for himself the condition of his subjects. Garcilaso shows him to us as a timorous man who did not dare to initiate any notable enterprise for fear of angering the Sun. But a certain kindness for the poor was perhaps sufficient reason for admiration. Huaman Poma judges him fairly in describing him as a peaceful king, a friend to the poor, a patient husband, and with a respect for humble customs. An epidemic threatened his people at the beginning of his reign, and he decided to undertake a long tour to maintain morale and to pay homage to the local gods. He stopped first at the *huacas,* the little shrines built alongside the roads or on the hills.

These shrines, as we know, were the homes of spirits and familiar gods. By extension, the name was applied to the magic power of the deities. But the origin of the shrines was the place where one groaned or shed tears to induce the spirits to be well-disposed and to frighten away the demons. Often important people were buried in them, even members of the dynasty, and a roughly shaped stone recalled the presence of the deceased. The very name of the king destined him to undertake this pilgrimage to the mystical sources of the country. The literal translation of Yahuar Huacac does not presage happiness, for it meant 'he who weeps blood . . .'

The first stage led the king, his wife, and their suite to a place called Huanacauri, two leagues distant from the capital. It may be recalled that one of Manco Capac's brothers was turned to stone there. A stela with human forms on it had been set in the ground, and the people of Cuzco came frequently to bring modest offerings of feathers, woollen garments, and fruits. The Inca meditated for a long time and then went on his way, stopping at all the shrines he encountered. Some represented the Creator, Thunder, or the Sun, others subterranean powers. Sometimes ten little boys or ten little girls were sacrificed in a shrine in the hope that the gods would be content with this gift and spare more precious lives (those of the executioners, for example). But Yahuar Huacac brought in his baggage a collection of gold statuettes, and he more often preferred to offer a reproduction of his young subjects rather than see them slaughtered. In this way he deprived his priests of the pleasure of daubing the faces of those present with the victims' blood, but he consoled them by dancing with them around the shrines.

When he returned from this journey, the annual September feast of the Citua took place in the presence of the queen, the princesses, and the wives of the nobility. The rainy season was approaching, and with it a recrudescence of people's ailments. At a time fixed by the astronomers as being the most favourable—doubtless the new moon—all the provincial visitors, all citizens who were sick, hunch-backed or in any way abnormal, were driven from the capital so as not to offend the goddess by the sight of their misfortunes. In the central square, soldiers armed with spears and slings faced to the four cardinal points and awaited the arrival of the king. When his litter appeared, borne by the princes of the blood and sur-rounded by priests, the sound of trumpets shattered the air. The soldiers replied by shouts and, brandishing their arms, they rushed in opposite directions. Whilst they went off as if pursuing an enemy, Yahuar Huacac poured a cup of maize *chicha* on the ground. The cries gradually died away and the silence told the king that, according to tradition, the warriors had plunged into the waters of the river Watanay to wash away all trace of illness. Out-side their houses the citizens took off their clothes and covered their bodies with a maize paste. They intoned a prayer to Viracocha: 'O Creator! let us live another year'. At dusk the king and the members of his family danced in the square until darkness fell on Cuzco once again. Only then did they return to the palace, and through a town deserted by its inhabitants a procession of priests carrying torches purified the streets and crossings. They beat the ground and the walls with their brands and then threw them into the river. Two leagues away from Cuzco, the infirm and the strangers to the city saw no other lights than those of the shining stars and knew that harmful spirits had fled, and they rejoiced in their hearts.

But Huaman Poma tells us that the king's family suffered from illness and several of his children died. In these cases the *Ichuri*, the doctor-priests, were not held responsible, nor was accident or infection. If the Inca dynasty, although protected by the Sun, was struck down by the ills which attacked other men, it was held to be due to irreligious practices amongst the king's entourage or even in the Empire itself (for instance, killing by means of sorcery). These breaches of the established order always aroused the anger of the gods, and the punishments were illness or death, and they threatened all the members of the community. The Inca himself, in spite of his supernatural origin and his immortality, ran the same risks, for during his time on earth he was the subordinate of the gods. He accepted his sufferings with humility, for they were, after all, an expression of justice. But he considered, as far as the law permitted, all measures which would remove the trials they constantly endured both from himself and his people. Offerings of gold and silver, and human sacrifices increased throughout the Empire, and its subjects were compelled to make confession.

This practice of confession was not confined to the Incas; the Chibchas of Colombia knew of it. If the Peruvians made frequent use of the confessional it was because they conceived it as a means of government or a police procedure. To begin with it was only an act which publicly recognised their sins and implored the indulgence of the gods. But it was also a curative medicine, for at the end of the confession the ills from which the penitent was suffering should have disappeared. The Spanish Fathers who came with the conquest and who saw only an immense caricature of Christianity in this custom did not realise that it was embedded in the spirit of Indian beliefs. The naked men of the Amazon trusted in the same system when they accused themselves before the chief of the tribe of having violated some taboo. As soon as illness or death are accepted as the automatic punishment for sin, an equally automatic pardon is expected if the necessary rites of purification are carried out. To the religious this may seem a conception of a sacrament which is far from spiritual. According to our European ideas, the Indian is always a shocking materialist!

At Cuzco, the high priest, the *Villac huma,* and in the villages the *Ichuri* settled themselves on the banks of rivers to await their sinful clients. In their right hands they held hanks of alfa grass and in their left, sticks with stone heads rather like clubs. The first of the penitents came forward a few steps and threw himself at the priest's feet, crying 'Hear me! Hear me!' The confessor raised him up saying that he already knew many of his sins, but he was ready to hear them from his own mouth. The confession began. The kneeling man was only a chief of ten families, a humble citizen, and the recital of his misdeeds taught the *Ichuri* nothing new about human weakness nor about the devices of the wealthy, the thieves, or the blasphemers. 'I have not given to the headman of the village the fruits which were his due. I ate them myself. I have not prayed to the Sun. I have not prayed to the Moon. I stole my neighbour's *coui* (Indian pig). I made love to his daughter'.

'How many times?' asked the *Ichuri*.

'Once, on the communal feast-day. I have not cultivated the king's land with the same energy that I have my own'.

'This is serious', said the priest. 'You know what punishments you will receive if your chief of fifty families hears of your laziness?'

'Alas! he could hang me. But have I not already been punished by Viracocha, with all these sores on my body?'

The confessor thought that the superior of this unfortunate man would come and in his turn accuse himself of negligence, and he sighed sadly. The one hundred strokes with the whip which these wretched peasants deserved would never be given because he, the priest, was bound by the secrecy of the confessional. He had only his stick with which to inflict punishment on the sinners. And he had to use this in moderation! All the same he beat the man's back as hard as his patriotic zeal allowed. Since he uttered no cry of distress, he began again, giving each of his blows a definite meaning—one for the offerings which had not been made, another for the forgotten prayers, and three or four (providing for lies and omissions) for the caresses. When he came to the lost hours of work, the peasant began to groan under the violence of the punishment. The *Ichuri,* thinking that the soil was sufficiently prepared to receive the seed, spoke of the majesty of the gods, the greatness of the Inca, and the goodness of *Villac huma.* Then he told the penitent to spit with him on the hank of alfa. 'Once more', he said in a gentler tone. It was a consoling sight, for the sins flashed out from the man's mouth with his saliva. 'Now bathe yourself', said the priest, and he threw the sin-ridden grass into the river. The ceremony was over. 'May the water carry the stains far away so that they never return'.

The peasant came out of the water shivering with fever. But as he went towards his home he saw his neighbour's daughter going to confession, and he was seized with a great desire to be healed for good.

At Cuzco the confessional ceremonies were more imposing, since many officials had a kinship with the royal family. Bodily weaknesses bordered on treason, and lust exercised against the princesses seems, strangely enough, to have been a crime against nature. Only the ears of the high priest might listen to such confessions. Of course wisdom recommended that only relatively venial sins should be revealed. 'I have made my uncle's skull into a jug to hold *chicha*. I have made a flute from my uncle's tibia. Whilst hunting I killed one of the llamas of the king's herd. I was drunk one day when I should have been at the confessional. I made a mistake when counting the knots on my *quipou*'. No doubt *Villac huma* thought all this very tiresome; he could not reveal the confessional secrets of a man who deserved death. 'Do you know what punishment you deserve?' he would murmur into an official's ear; 'a stone round your neck and a jump into eternity—or at least imprisonment outside Cuzco'.

If the penitent had some major sin to confess, he would certainly think of the 'other' prison, a cave full of wild beasts, snakes and spiders, where the condemned were subjected for two days to the most terrible judgment of the gods that the Inca mind had devised. But some sinners did have the courage to own up to sins which assured them the road to the cave. On these the priest imposed, as a penance, the necessity of denouncing themselves before the king's justice.

The confessional period ended, and the shrines honoured according to tradition, Cuzco resumed its working life. Each day a llama clad in red—the Inca's colour—was sacrificed and prayers were said to the god, begging him 'never to grow old, and to rise each day to bring light to the world'. Those who had not recovered their health were placed in the category of incurable, number four in the population plan. All they could do was to make use of such medicine as there was to alleviate their sufferings.

In the villages, the *sancoyoc*, the sorcerers, diagnosed illness and ordered treatment. They often carried out the treatment themselves, making their attentions more agreeable by invocations, trances, suctions, and other proceedings familiar to all magicians.

Fig. 36. Sorcerers at work

They then said that they were entered by the spirit of a bird, a stone, or the colour of the sky. But their true strength lay in a sound knowledge of healing. If they were unable to obtain the necessary products on the spot, from the *Hampi Camayoc,* the keepers of remedies authorised by law, they awaited the arrival of the *Colla-huaya,* the travelling chemists of the Empire, who had in their wallets the essential medicinal plants, and doubtless, amulets acquired in the course of their travels, such as lime stones, stag's horns, shells, and bezoards.[1]

The early Spanish historians have recorded in very great detail comparative lists of Inca illnesses and remedies. They show that the Peruvians took care of their health and that in certain respects they were more skilful and better informed than their contemporaries in Europe. All the same, the skulls which we are able to study today scarcely inspire us with confidence, for the greater number of them show traces of a defective diet and a short life. In truth, life at great altitudes was the permanent tragedy of the Incas. Without abundant food and adequate shelter, man was threatened with a rapid weakening of his strength, and diseases which were mild in other places were deadly in the Andes. The peasants cried out in terror, *'Kaikar! kaikar!'* when they began to cough on returning from a journey. They thought that the breath of dead men had entered their bodies, and simple bronchitis might bring them to the grave. The malignant air was to them the origin of the most varied ills—eczema, nettle-rash, tetanus, lumbago, and even epilepsy. Add to this list pneumonia, marsh fever, congestion of the brain, intestinal disorders, dropsy, and finally verruga, epidemics of which even today are common in parts of the Andes. All these ailments had names in the Quechua tongue, and all were treated with some kind of remedy.

The best known was quinine; *quina quina* the Indians called it. It was used for dressing wounds and to abate fever.[2] Sores and wounds were a major preoccupation with a conquering people, and one loses count of all the plants used by the Peruvians to treat them. There were at least ten of these growing near Cuzco alone, and of

[1] A stony substance which forms in the stomachs of animals. The bezoard of a tapir is the most sought after.
[2] Quinine: *Myroxilon peruiferum.* Juan Lopez de Canizara, at Loxa in Peru, was cured of a raging fever by quinine, and he sent a parcel of this bark to Spain in 1638. At the same time Pedro Barbia published the first account of the properties of quinine. Later Jussieu, W. Arrot, and above all La Conda-mine made use of 'bark from Loxa'.

these *Pacha Toya* mixed with salt and white of egg was used to treat fractures. Wild barley cured ulcers (and killed lice), the bark of *ratanhia,* which contained tannin, cured dysentery; *chilca*[1] was given to those suffering from lung trouble and rheumatism, the juice and pips of tropical fruits cured eye affections, toothache, or skin eruptions. Emetics and purgatives were provided, as well as herbs to ease childbirth or miscarriages. According to Santacruz Pachacuti, lustful old men had the right to a piece of *huarnarpo,*[2] which, according to the chroniclers, helped them to become adulterers. They made use of prescriptions to mitigate the ravages of syphilis, which was rampant in the north of the country and which poets say was transmitted to men by llamas. Although the chroniclers are guarded, it is believed that sulphate of copper and a powder with a base of sulphuretted arsenic, *huaini-hampi* was used to alleviate syphilitic ulcers and sores, at least superficially.

To the remedies of vegetable or mineral origin, the Incas added a *materia medica* of animal origin, such as dove's heart to stop hæmorrhage, condor blood for nervous troubles, llama blood for attacks of *kaikar,* skunk blood for congestions, fat of jaguar, condor, and bear for swellings. A *Colla-huaya* was even known to have provided an ointment of human fat. Living animals were also made to contribute: small snakes that the goitrous were obliged to eat in the hope that the protuberances would disappear, and especially large ants which were called 'the Inca's hooks and eyes' because of their manner of usage. Cobo relates that these insects were placed on wounds in such a way that they bit the two lips of the wound; their heads were then cut off, their claws retained a tight hold, and a real suture resulted. Here was a surgical practice that leads us to the consideration of an art or science of which the Incas were masters.

The peasants often had to seek the help of surgeons. The *sancoyoc* of the village was able to treat a fracture, open an abscess, or extract a tooth. The imperial doctors were reserved for the king's armies and the highest officers of the capital. The Inca hierarchy was applied even in the matter of broken limbs. This is easily understood if ever one has the opportunity to hold in one's own hand a trepanned skull—the masterpiece of Peruvian surgery. We should not have the bad taste to wax lyrical about a frontal or occipital

[1] *Baccharis lanceolata.*
[2] *Jatropha basiacantha.* (Pax and K. Hoffman.)

bone pierced by a hole, but Broca exhibited once and for all the enthusiasm of scholars and others when he studied the superb example brought from Cuzco in 1860 by the American Squier. It must be said that this was a specially chosen skull, a worthy study for posterity, with its little skylight cut in the upper part of the skull. Since then hundreds of skulls, especially those studied by Dr. Tello, showed rectangular, polygonal, round or oval openings, with varying techniques. The Inca surgeons, who were always trying to find ways of improving their method of operation, used several instruments to this end: first the flint or obsidian knife,[1] then the *tumi*, a semi-circular blade of bronze held by a central handle, then metal scalpels like the *champi*, with a gold, copper, or silver handle. Thus, either by scraping the bone, or cutting it, or making little peripheral holes, which would then produce a scalloped hole in the skull, the Peruvians gained access to the mysterious world of the brain.

Why did they trepan skulls? The Incas are silent and the motives which inspired them are a matter for conjecture. 'Magic!' cried Broca. Epilepsy and fits of all kinds terrified primitive peoples, and in this way the idea of possession was born—only a spirit which was imprisoned in a human body could produce such effects. Open a door and the demon would fly away! This would be the magical origin of an operation which little by little became a religious manifestation. Dominique Wölfel retorts that it was a simple surgical operation designed to relieve soldiers wounded in the head by clubs or sling missiles. Tello replies that it was a reasonable treatment applied to fractures of the skull, infectious bone inflammations, and bone lesions caused by syphilis. These opinions are less opposed to one another than would appear at first sight. The magic origin of trepanning cannot be doubted, and it is certain that the Incas made use of it for practical ends. In this they remained faithful to their utilitarian conception of life.

As to the operation itself, carried out with an evident regard for antisepsis, it is difficult to know what proportion of operations was successful. The skull studied by Broca shows a survival of from ten to fifteen days, but others are more optimistic and allow a few extra years of life to the patient. The patient!—that is indeed the most

[1] With a flint knife 'found on the quays of the Seine', Lucas Championière, in 1878, performed the same trepanning operation as the Incas in thirty minutes.

suitable word to use for the one who undergoes the operation, judging by the scene which adorns the handle of the *tumi* in the illustration.

Fig. 37. Tumi, a trepanning instrument, with decoration showing operation in progress

CHAPTER IX

THE ADVENTURES OF KING VIRACOCHA

Doubts about the faithfulness of a queen. Viracocha, the phantom prince, routs rebellious tribes–The temple with the twelve corridors–Conquest of the country of the Diaguites

☐

FOR an Indian father, beardless and with a yellow skin, it is tiresome to have a son with a pale skin and a beard. But for the king of the Incas, uncompromising about the purity of royal blood, it is an infinitely greater misfortune. Here is the description given by Huaman Poma of one of the three sons of Yahuar Huacac. 'A man with a white body and with a slight beard', the legend has it.

Fig. 38.
One of the three sons of Yahuar Huacac

In these ancient times, children who were abnormal in any way were considered to be the offspring of spirits, such as those of the rainbow or thunder—or at least negligence on the part of the parents had made way for the intervention of these evil spirits.

Amongst the reproaches which the parents exchanged on these occasions, the most violent were directed against the father, who evidently had not fasted during his wife's pregnancy. This magic dietary rule was so important that after the birth of the little monstrosity, the parents abstained from eating pepper—a judicious precaution which restrained their ardour—though rather belatedly. We do not know if Yahuar Huacac was the recipient of such remonstrances on the part of his queen, the slender lady Ipauacoma. We think not. The Inca's majesty was sufficient to protect him from criticism, and besides, the constant presence of his concubines gave him, in relation to the *Coya*,[1] that fulfilment and serenity known only to those practising polygamy. On his side, did the king question his wife precisely about her possible lovers? It is easy to imagine her more preoccupied with her tame parrots and performing monkeys than with her young male friends, but Huaman Poma says she was obliged 'to protect herself from men'. Is this the key to this little mystery? And if so, who was the queen's partner?

The chroniclers do not answer this question. The Inca kings were to them superior beings whose actions and feelings they only considered in relation to their function as it affected the interest of the state. Only that sharp-nosed old Huaman Poma raised the veil that covered the face of the son of the Son. He does not say that Yahuar Huacac had been made a figure of fun, but what he does tell us, when compared with the historical accounts, allows us to imagine the adulterous origin of the young man. The first objection that could be raised is that Peruvian law itself was very severe in the matter of extra-marital relations; the guilty ones were whipped, or if they belonged to an honoured official class, they were tied together by the hair and hung from the rocks. This punishment, and those which governed rape and crimes of passion, applied to the Inca's subjects and not to the royal family. Was the queen's infidelity punished even more severely? Those who see order and virtue in the rule of the Inca Empire say she was. But the sceptics say the kings had their own ethics. And it appears that these observers who had no illusions were right. Huaman, in the summary he gives of the life of the Inca queens, attributes to them a fairly free life, with friends and personal riches, the right to dispose of their wealth as they saw fit, and finally an important part in the pattern of religious life, since they presided at the ceremonies connected with the wor-

[1] The Star. This name was given to the legitimate wife of the king.

ship of the Moon. One can see no similarity between their lives and those of the wives of the common people. Were they not sisters to the kings before becoming their wives? And even at the founding of the Empire, Mama Ocllo had her own quarter, or at least her own personal residence at Cuzco. The *Coya* had power and personal liberty which were certainly greater than was accorded to her by the historians, who were somewhat obsessed by the 'despotic' character of the regime. We must not forget that in South America women have often held command (and they were not always kindly rulers!). The illegal loves of the Inca queens, however sacrilegious they may have been, rank as possibilities.

The second objection concerns the hairy appearance of the son of Ipauacoma. Is this an established fact? The much criticised portrait of the prince is the keystone of our argument. We have every reason for confidence in the drawings of the Indian chronicler, whose source of information was the portrait gallery of the royal ancestors—several witnesses guarantee the authenticity of this. The Spanish historians did not attach much importance to it, but their accounts of this period often allude to beards and to people with fair skins. This is the key to the affair—but we must not anticipate.

Yahuar Huacac did not care for his son, whom he considered quarrelsome and undisciplined; he broke idols and wanted to set fire to the temples. Garcilaso wrote: 'The Inca, not knowing what to do, exiled him and resolved to disinherit him. He planned to put in his place another of his children who would not disgrace the morality of his ancestors'. The young man was sent to guard the herd of the Sun, some leagues from Cuzco. The king took pleasure in this banishment, but three years later his son presented himself at the palace and demanded to see his father. Yahuar Huacac fell into a violent rage, for it was midday and therefore the sacred hour when there were no shadows, an hour which was sacred throughout the Empire of the Sun. Besides it was time for the midday meal.

'Tell my son that I will have him killed for his disobedience'. But the prince forced his way into the royal apartments and immediately plunged into his story.

'Whilst resting half asleep under a rock in the pasture of Chita, a man appeared before me. His face was very different from ours, for he had a long beard. A robe covered him from head to foot and he had an unknown animal on a lead. He said to me, "My nephew, I am a son of the Sun and brother of Manco Capac and Mama

Ocllo. My name is Viracocha Inca. I have come to give you an important warning which you must convey to your father. The northern provinces which are subject to the Empire and some others which are not are conspiring together to overthrow the dynasty and the city of Cuzco. But I will help you in your troubles—you can depend on my aid". I set out at once', added the prince, 'to tell you of this event'.

The king was silent a few moments and then expressed his august opinion. 'My son is mad', he said. 'Let him go and watch his llamas and not trouble me any more with these tales of apparitions'.

Unhappy Yahuar Huacac. Some months later, the Chanca, Vilca, and Uramarca tribes rebelled and killed the Inca officials, and soon their army of 30,000 strong was approaching the capital. The king consulted the soothsayers, but obtaining no favourable reply from the gods, decided to abandon Cuzco. His son hurried after him and demanded an audience a second time. But his tone had changed.

'Can it be that you are so ill-advised as to abandon your city and your house? For my part I will not agree and I will go and perish amongst the enemy before they enter Cuzco! Follow me who will!'

These proposals, no doubt slightly embroidered by the perceptive Garcilaso, appealed to the dignitaries of the court, the more so because Yahuar Huacac gave evident signs of mental weakness. Four thousand men answered the prince's call, and they named him after the bearded spirit—Viracocha Inca. The eighth sovereign was virtually chosen even before the death of his predecessor—a unique event in the history of the Peruvian dynasty which must be especially noted.

Viracocha sounded the call to arms of all the forces available— the faithful Quechuas, the brave Aymaras, and all those from the south and east. They rallied in great numbers—the old ones happy to renew the tradition of fighting campaigns, the young delighted to exchange spades for clubs. In a few days the prince had 20,000 men at his disposal, and the chronicler says: 'he attributed this happy outcome to his uncle the apparition'. Perhaps he had him by his side to advise him! In any case, the years passed in watching the herds had not impaired his innate flair for strategy. He placed his troops partly on a plain and partly on the heights. A force of 5,000 soldiers was held in reserve under the lee of a hill. When the enemy came to give battle he sent messengers of peace, according to custom, but they were received with insults. The Inca had the trumpets sounded and the first shower of bronze missiles opened the way for the foot soldiers. Men fell, blood—a precious seed—flowed over the ground. But cries of rage drowned the groans. 'Sutio, Sutio,' roared Viracocha's men, as if to summon their sacred spirit to their aid. At the beginning of the afternoon the outcome of the battle was uncertain and the reserve was thrown in. They charged the Chancas' right wing, which withdrew and was taken in the rear by the detachments posted on the heights. From this moment the day was won. Last-minute reinforcements, the Cuzco officials united under a new leader, joined the combatants to take part in the final massacre—and they were no less cruel than the rest. At sunset Viracocha crossed the battlefield and halted near a river—its waters were red. Thirty thousand dead were counted, says Garcilaso. This place was afterwards called Yahuarpampa, the plain of blood. Yahuar Huacac, the king with blood-red tears, was forgotten.

After the victory, Viracocha received the homage of the capital. He showed himself at the head of his troops, and scorning the royal palanquin, he advanced like a war leader should, his arms in his hand, and covered with dust. Excited by the strident call of the trumpets and the beating of the drums, the crowd threw down sweet herbs and sang songs of joy. The soldiers filed past, and then the prisoners, upon whom they poured jeers. Behind them came the officials who had taken part in the last hours of the battle, and then the princesses carried in litters. In the midst of the central square the queen, Ipauacoma, awaited her son. She bowed as if to salute him as the legitimate king and conducted him to the temple of the Sun. There he cast off his shoes and was present whilst a llama was sacrificed. Viracocha ended this triumphal day by visiting the aclahuasi, the house of the chosen women. The prettiest girls in the Empire, chosen each year by special officials, spinning and chatting, there awaited the good pleasure of the princes. Those who composed the upper class—the most beautiful—were destined for the service of the Sun. They remained virgins until the king decided to deflower them in the name of the Sun. Otherwise they would serve in the temple or take care of the young newcomers, unless the Inca offered them to his victorious captains.

One of the first acts of the reign of Viracocha was to build a temple sixteen leagues from Cuzco. It is known that he dedicated it to his namesake [1] and that the statue, representing him in the same attitude as that of the apparition, 'resembled those of the apostles and especially that of Saint Bartholomew, who is usually shown trampling an evil spirit underfoot'. This phrase of Garcilaso's raises for the second time the question of Europeans in pre-

Fig. 39.
Diaguites
pottery

Columbian America, but no scientific value can really be accorded to this, any more than to the 'giants' as the builders of a very old town at Tiahuanaco. It simply shows that men with fair skins and some sort of beard reached the Peruvian Empire at this time and enjoyed a certain amount of influence at the Inca court. It is probable that they were Indians of a slightly different race: Chimus who came from the north coast of Peru and who, we know, used hair tweezers [2] of gold; or they may have been ordinary pilgrims from distant regions of Colombia or Central America, bringing new beliefs with them. Beliefs but no skills—no pottery, no wheel, no writing. If Europeans of the 14th century had been in Peru, they would certainly have influenced the material life of the Incas, who were always eager for progress. There is nothing in the accession of Viracocha and the setting aside of the dynastic law to lend support to the idea of intervention of men of foreign blood. The Empire was saved—is not this the most consoling thing about this story?

The eighth ruler extended his territory towards the south, and

[1] See Part One, Chapter II.
[2] Near Moche, on the coast north of Lima, a statue of a bearded man has been found.

crossing the Andes, penetrated into the country of the Diaguites, on the edge of the Argentine plain. Fortunately he did not have to give battle against these Indians, who were renowned for their courage and their skill in combat. Their fortresses, standing on the heights, were opened to the Inca envoys, and their incendiary arrows remained in their quivers. The Peruvians admired the fine pottery and funerary urns of the Diaguites. They visited their temples and were present at their human sacrifices. Many of their customs were

*Fig. 40.
Diaguites
funerary
urn*

surprising—isolation of sick people by a circle of arrows, the trances of the rain-makers, the carved pipes which the old men passed round during their councils, the young people's initiation ceremonies and the orgiastic feasts which followed. But what most astonished the Peruvians was the advanced system of agriculture, with terraced fields and artificial irrigation, a domain in which they themselves were experts. They had only to bring the methods of their new allies to perfection by teaching them, for example, to build aqueducts and canals. These works were the pride of the Incas, and Viracocha, during a rapid expedition into the northern province, ordered the construction of a canal one hundred leagues long and nine to twelve feet deep, which would bring water to the fields and pastures of the central zone. Springs and glacier lakes fed this irrigation system, whose supply was controlled by artificial reserves. At times mountains had to be outflanked or traversed by a tunnel (as the one near Cajamarca). But nothing stopped the Peruvians, who took pleasure in struggling with natural obstacles. These canals of hewn stone rivalled in perfection the Empire's paved roads. And it was to the credit of Viracocha that he brought as a gift to the newest of his subjects the means of making the most of their own country. It is true that in return he imposed his laws, his controllers and his judges, without of course forgetting his recruiting officers.

During his reign Viracocha made several tours of his Empire. His legitimate wife consoled herself with dwarfs and hunchbacks during his absences, and also made use of coca to excess. But one cannot reproach a king for neglecting his home for affairs of state, and in any case they had many children.

CHAPTER X

CONQUEST AND FAME

The greatest century of the Empire-Selected thoughts of king Pacha-cutec-Justice-Cuzco is rebuilt—The fortress and the 'tired stone'—The god Pachacamac enters the Inca pantheon

□

IT was now the 15th century. Paris had 200,000 inhabitants, scarcely double the number of Cuzco. Joan of Arc delivered Orleans; Gutenberg set up the type of the first printed Bible. Europe was daily striving and working to obtain a little more freedom. And in Peru . . .

Yacha huasi was not only a college reserved for the princes; it had become the school of administration for the Empire. There was a passing-out examination, the *huaraku,* in which the highest marks were given for physical and military exercises. After six days of a diet of pure water and crushed maize, and a trial of nervous resistance to the threat of clubs, the young candidates had to manoeuvre and give battle. They had also to answer questions about religion, the sciences, and political economy. Those with the highest marks received their heavy earrings, the insignia of the ruling caste, from the king. The ninth ruler, Pachacutec the Reformer, himself presided at the distribution of these diplomas which were both showy and elegant. The newly promoted threw themselves at his feet and awaited the speech which would be their guide for the rest of their lives. The king stood up in the midst of the crowd of professors, priests and soldiers. He was tall and muscular, and his intimates say that he had the eyes of a lion. His voice was strong, and he said, 'If one cannot count the knots of a *quipou,* it is folly to want to count the stars'. He reseated himself on his stone chair; having delivered his message, it was for the young men to meditate upon it. All Cuzco was aware of the king's liking for sententious phrases and the officials slavishly repeated them several times a day, taught them to their children, and woke up at night to recount them to their wives. In this way, without the help of any written manuscript, the words of the Reformer have come down to us. Here are a few chosen examples .

'If you are unable to keep your family in order, what would you do in affairs of state?'

'The peace of a nation comes from the obedience of all its subjects'.

'The chiefs must be indulgent to the fearful. For braggarts, punishments must be severe'.

'Judges who accept presents must be treated as thieves'.

'In a well-organised state it is just to hang cowards; otherwise they become thieves'.

'Adultery is like theft : its punishment must be death'.

'A man condemns himself to death when he kills without authority'.

'Rage denotes a weak character'.

'Jealousy is a worm which gnaws at a man's vitals'.

'Jealousy is like a spider which draws its poison from the most beautiful flowers'.

These reflections of Pachacutec were not the basis of a new moral code, but they recalled the five essential prohibitions of the Inca law : lying, laziness, theft, murder and debauchery.

The king liked to use imagery in his pronouncements because the headmen, dealing with minor offences, and the *Tucuy ricoc,* the governors and provincial judges, remembered them as easily as the refrain of a song. In the task of control and unification rendered necessary by the expansion of the Empire, and also because of a certain amount of laxity on the part of the officials, the first care of the sovereign was to ensure an uncompromising justice. No infraction of the laws was allowed to go unpunished, but the procedure respected the rights of the accused. Pachacutec saw to this personally and very often informed himself about the conduct of cases.

The theft of fruits or maize was reported to the chief of ten families and he informed the headman. Immediately a meeting was called, and the old men, the witnesses, and the chiefs of ten families in the village surrounded the accused. Women were not allowed as witnesses because they were 'deceitful and untruthful by nature', nor were the poor, for they 'were easier to bribe than the rich', according to Huaman Poma. If the accused pleaded guilty, judgment was pronounced on the spot. If guilt was not proved, the headman ordered a further enquiry. In the case of theft of fruits or maize, the most important thing was to know who had been the

Fig. 41. Punishment of an adulterous woman

victim—a peasant or the king. To steal a part of the harvest destined for the king was punishable with death. A theft from the priests merited so many blows with a stick—several hundred—that the condemned man died by the end of the punishment. The tenacity of the accused in defending themselves can be well understood, for if they did not establish their innocence they could at least appeal to the Sun, the Moon, and their ancestors' mummies. This meant yielding to the judgment of the gods. This only delayed sentence, for if the evidence was strong, a few minutes' torture produced a plea of guilty. Convicted of having stolen the Inca's goods, the wretched man was thrown into a ravine or hung by the heels.

Satisfied with his criminal justice and eager to have it respected, Pachacutec undertook the task of applying the economic laws in such a way as to strengthen the Empire. The aim of all reform was to produce more. The gravest obstacle was the diversity of languages spoken in the Four Corners of Tawantinsuyu. The controllers from Cuzco had tried in vain to learn the Aymara, Calchaki, Nasca, and Chuncho dialects, and many others; they could not keep up with the task, for the peasants showed themselves confused and yet respectful. Mistakes were easily made about ploughing, sowing, and division of harvests, especially when they were not very anxious to understand words involving taxation! Pachacutec then resolved to extend the use of the Quechua tongue throughout the Empire. It is a supple language, rich in composite words the meaning of which varied according to the affixes, and permitting expression of the most abstract ideas and also of all shades of doubt and certainty. The language of conquerors and poets! First the king decreed that no important office should be given to anyone who did not speak Quechua; then he sent schoolmasters throughout the provinces and called together to Cuzco, for a course, the sons of the principal chiefs who had recently surrendered. But he did not limit himself to these measures. From the villages near the capital he chose groups of families whom he despatched to distant territories, charged with the double duty of learning the tongue of the natives and teaching them Quechua. Until this time the Incas had used this method of displacement of the population only when they wished to bring an uninhabited region into production, but now it became a permanent custom, even a political system. Loyal tribes were transplanted to assist in policing conquered territories. The experiment proving decisive, the exchanges were intensified to the point that the

Mitimaes, 'the people who are sent elsewhere', were sometimes entrusted with a military mission—that of defending the frontiers. Then they were amongst the privileged class and received presents from Cuzco and wives to keep them company. But on the whole, the situation of the displaced families was pitiable, for the Peruvian Indian, having lost all initiative with the passing of the centuries, was happy only on his ancestors' patch of ground.

Pachacutec completed his work of unification by laws which regulated work with great precision, established compulsory military training, and reduced the standard of living of the people to the lowest point. No more feather ornaments or clothes of vicuña wool, no more simmering dishes, one drink only—maize *chicha*. This hopeless austerity is today called basic levelling. To Garcilaso, who at times finds quite delightful expressions, 'it was the means of blocking the road to the corruption which luxury and superfluous expenditure have a habit of inducing'. Besides, adds the chronicler, 'to prevent continual work from making the Indians discontented, the king ordered three days' public holiday at each new moon'. This grand manner does not give colour to the monotonous and laborious Inca universe which Pachacutec finally brought to perfection.

One could wish that the ruler had applied to himself and his family the same high principles which he imposed on his people. But unfortunately, our conception of political ethics is as liable to great disappointment amongst the Incas as amongst ourselves—perhaps more so. Pachacutec, like his great-grandfather Roca, was scornful of sentimental possibilities. He had an Asiatic conception of perfection—the people were perfect because they did not aspire to be anything more than the people, but he himself would be only a true king if he possessed absolute power and supreme renown. He already had power; but fame, together with stupidity, is the most painful of human passions in the sense that perfection can never be reached in either. Pachacutec, however, set out to attain fame. He decided to rebuild Cuzco so that it would be worthy of its place as the imperial capital.

The *amautas,* who were expert in architecture, the *sayu-choctasuyoc,* who were the surveyors, and the guilds of craftsmen concerned with city building, under orders from the king, drew up in relief a plan for the future city. Buildings such as the palace of Roca and Viracocha, the school of administration, and the convent of the chosen women would be kept, and the temple of the Sun enlarged. But the majority of the other houses would be pulled down. Pachacutec accepted these suggestions and to ease the task of the builders, he sent away all the inhabitants whose presence was not absolutely necessary and settled them outside the town. Fifty thousand men set to work. The names of their leaders are unknown,

Fig. 42. Peruvian builders

which is a pity, for not only was their town a masterpiece of simplicity, but their new technique revolutionised classical Indian architecture. Until this time, walls were built of polygonal blocks of stone, which were fitted but irregular. The builders of the 'Pachacutec style' made use of square or rectangular stones, carefully cut and fixed with such precision that one could not insert a pin point between them. The effect was severe but much more harmonious. The doors were higher, windows better designed, and the roof, sloping in each direction, no longer ran the risk of being blown in during storms.[1] Inside, niches were provided for domestic objects, pots of ointment, and for statuettes of the gods of the family hearth whose worship was becoming widespread. On the walls were tiles of gold or silver.

[1] Wiener distinguishes four periods in the architecture. Megalithic, huge roughly dressed stone, small roughly dressed stone, and rectangular polygonal stone. This last period really corresponds with the Pachacutec style, and the stones used were rectangular, flat, and polished on all four faces.

The central square was itself improved. The rushing torrent of the Watanay was covered with broad flagstones in such a way that religious ceremonies or military parades could be displayed in all their majesty. When the works were completed, the king assembled his officials at the entrance to the city. He showed them on the plan the spot where they should settle themselves, and gave them the title of citizens. Then he turned his thoughts to another project which was in process of realisation and which would impress everyone with his military renown. This was the fortress of Sacsahuaman.

Almost every day the king's litter climbed the road to the northwest of the city and halted on the huge plateau which overlooked the valley. Thousands of men were toiling in the yellow dust, scorched by the sun; they were putting stones into position. But some of the blocks of stone were nine feet high, taller than their own huts, and they weighed five to ten tons. These figures are as eloquent as the exclamations of the idlers, faced with the amazing spectacle of this human anthill. On artificial ramps with a gentle slope, gangs of a hundred men at a time were dragging up roughly hewn blocks, with the aid of aloe-fibre ropes. The top of a ramp reached the upper part of the wall under construction. When the stone had been brought to the top, a foreman directed its siting and had its roughness levelled in such a way that it could be fitted exactly to the neighbouring blocks. Then the rock was raised with huge wooden levers, and a mass of arms and backs pushed with all their might and all their despair. For if the fibre ropes which held the stone up gave way, everyone would have been crushed. Each year several fathoms were added to the height and extent of the walls. Pachacutec completed the front which overlooked the town, and the first two outer enclosures which were six hundred feet long and protected the opposite side. Access was by two narrow gateways, one at ground level, 'the gateway of sand', and the other in the upper level, 'the gateway of Achuana', the name of the architect. When the last wall was completed, the third gateway would be named Viracocha. Already the fortress offered remarkable protection with its three inner towers, built to withstand any siege. There the Inca had his houses, the Sun his temple, and there was a permanent water supply, brought from the mountains by underground conduits. Sacsahuaman sprang from Peruvian history, and neither time, wars, nor earthquakes have brought it low. It remains a witness to the strength of the Peruvian Empire.

But we must turn aside to understand with what infinite patience this famous citadel was erected. Pachacutec often traversed in his litter the hilly roads by which the stones were dragged to the site. The quarries were five or six leagues away. Sometimes a huge rock was abandoned—the efforts of the workers, yoked to their burden, could not overcome the mountain, and the king made enquiries about the reasons for this setback. But he was not severe with the workmen; it was the stone itself which wearied and could not reach its goal. Like his subjects he called this mass of granite that lay on the ground by a name full of affection—*saycusca,* the weary stone.

A people united by common laws and language, a noble capital, a strong fighting force—the king lacked no signs of majesty around him. But Pachacutec dreamed of an even greater honour—to offer a new divinity to the Empire. Once again chance favoured him. His brother, head of the armies, returned to Cuzco after a victorious campaign to the north and east. At the same time as the triumphal celebrations the tests of *Huaraku* took place, and the heir to the throne, Yupanqui, aged sixteen, came first in the trials. Here was a double family celebration for the sovereign! The General thus honoured took a fancy to his nephew and proposed to take him with him on an expedition of some interest. The plan was to push northward towards Cajamarca, a region said to be very rich and thickly populated, and then to subdue the whole coast as far as the country of the Yuncas, who worshipped the powerful god Irma. This enterprise attracted the king, but when he learned of its magnitude he decided to carry it out in two parts. First to go north and remove all threats from the Cordilleras, and then to go towards the sandy coast, where conditions necessitated special preparations for the struggle.

More than 50,000 men set out and quickly reached the region of the Hayllas, which had been subdued during the preceding campaign. When the general drew near the town he warned the young prince of the effeminate character of the inhabitants. 'Keep away from the Hayllas!' he said, laughing. This warning against the homosexuals was handed on to posterity as a proverb. Difficulties began with the Huaras people, who had to be reduced by starvation. With the Huamachucos, who worshipped stones at the edges of streams and made human sacrifices to them, a little diplomacy was all that was required. Now they had reached the borders of the

Cajamarca country. According to custom, the Inca general sent emissaries to demand surrender. But these Indians had been warned of the arrival of the army from Cuzco and were ready to defend themselves. War was thus inevitable; it lasted four months and claimed many victims. The enemy were in control of all the passes, and after a fight they retreated into fortresses which were difficult of access and built in such a way that they could communicate with one another by signals. Another danger threatened the Incas—the length of their lines of communication. They were about twelve hundred miles from Cuzco, and the state granaries were not enough to supply a vast army. But the General and Prince Yupanqui forced a decision by attacking the strongholds one after another, and on the plain defeated the rearguard of the people of Cajamarca. Then they made peace and entered the capital of this new country. When they saw the palaces and the riches they contained, they realised what a great prize they had taken.

Returning from this campaign, they crossed a high desert plateau on the left bank of the river Marañon and descended to the bottom of a circle of mountains. Here they saw a dark-coloured lake, the Lauricocha. To cross the torrent which flowed from it they built a stone bridge—plain blocks as a base, with flags laid across. They encamped at the foot of a great cliff excavated into galleries where, said the peasants, gnomes who were blacksmiths had lived in times gone by. The Inca general left some experts behind to look for minerals, and in so doing, an officer of Pachacutec's army made his way up the stream, rounded seven lakes, and one day found himself faced by a wall of glaciers which shut in the horizon. Without knowing it, he had reached, at a height of nearly fifteen thousand feet, the sources of the Amazon.

A triumphal and almost delirious reception awaited the conquering army. For a long time the runners had brought news of their exploits, and the new town resounded with cries of *hailli* and the sound of trumpets and songs of victory. The ceremonies lasted a month but this universal celebration did not affect the king. To him new lands meant roads to build, officials to appoint, and a system of production to establish. Battles were only the poetry of conquest; the real victory came to fruition in the half-light of the houses of Cuzco. It took three years to set in train the administrative and executive machinery which would ensure the assimilation of the conquered tribes, which meant that it was three years before

Pachacutec could despatch an expedition to seek out the god Irma. For this he prepared a powerful army with an entirely new set-up. He had 40,000 men divided into four autonomous corps, each one equipped with a complete armament and commissariat, and divided into units of 1,150 soldiers. The general, his brother, had warned him that the hard climate on the coast and the diversity of the enemy peoples, called for frequent relief for the troops engaged in action. Only in the event of grave emergency would they act together.

The campaign went as planned. The army reached the sandy plains on the coast near the town of Ica and marched towards the north. The Chincha tribes offered little resistance, or were subdued by the favourite Inca tactic: that of eight days siege followed by an offer of peace. In repeating this stratagem as often as possible, Pachacutec's ambassadors had the same attraction to the besieged, who were now reduced to famine, as a spring of clear water or a maize loaf. The people of Huarcu, on the contrary, fought for eight months and inflicted considerable losses on their assailants. But in the end they gave in, and their defeat opened the road to the celebrated valley of Rimac, and later the road to the deity.

Rima, 'he who speaks', was an idol whom the Indian chiefs consulted before hunting or going to war. Their oracles were known in the Cordilleras, and the Incas had no difficulty in adopting them. But the possession of the temple of Irma, the object of the military campaign, was the subject of discussion, and terms were agreed whereby the representatives of Cuzco and those of the local king each agreed to respect the gods of his adversary. Viracocha holding out a hand to Irma! Irma must be singularly powerful! He was especially very old.[1] But whilst Viracocha was the creator of all things and consequently took precedence over all things, Irma was descended from the Sun and Moon. His adherents recounted many wondrous stories, in particular his quarrels with the Sun, which were the occasion for the destruction of the first men. They affirmed that it was after this that Irma became invisible, in order to escape paternal rage. He also quarrelled with Kon, the Chimu-god, and pursued him into the sea. Then of his own accord he created a new race of men. This creation was not lacking in originality, for it was brought about by means of three eggs: a golden egg for nobles of

[1] The German archeologist Max Uhle makes the first period of civilisation in this region to coincide with the oldest period of Tiahuanaco.

the male sex, a silver egg for nobles of the female sex, and a copper egg for either sex of the common people. This hierarchy, applied to the cosmic egg, delighted the Incas. But when they entered the temple, having climbed the promontory which looked over the sea and the green valley of the Lurin, they were surprised by the poverty of the sacred place. The face of the god had been crudely carved in wood and was stained by the blood of thousands of sacrifices. Was this the god who controlled the harvests and whose counsels guided men in the paths of wisdom? They considered that Irma was not as great as Viracocha and they found him a name more suited to his worth—Pachacamac—made up of *pacha* the world, and *camac,* he who cares.

In this way, Pachacutec, the world reformer, introduced the god Pachacamac, the world saviour, to the pantheon of the Peruvian gods. His renown was complete. But having learned from his captains that the Chimu tribes, with their divinity Kon, would be an easy conquest, he made ready for a fourth military campaign. He was an insatiable ruler, as eager for the fame of his Empire as for his own. When he died, the people forgot his harsh laws, the austerity of their lives, and the graves on the battlefields, and they mourned for their king.

CHAPTER XI

THE FFAST OF THE SUN

A love song—The astrono.ners announce the summer solstice—The king welcomes his father the Sun—Sacrifice in the temple of the Curiancha —A popular holiday

□

THE queen raised a silver mirror to eye level. Around her the ladies of her suite, who were of a discreet age, awaited the verdict of their mistress. Was she satisfied with her shining and perfumed hair, with the blue veil lightly placed behind her head, with her soft orange-coloured woollen cape? Mama Ocllo, wife of the tenth ruler, was of a kindly disposition, but very punctilious about her appearance. She was pretty in spite of her small figure—sufficiently rounded to invite caresses. But the queen did not seek to enchant any man but the king, Tupac Yupanqui. She was even jealous, it was said, of the concubines whom her august husband chose from the young girls of the sacred house. In vain he explained that he had found no pleasure in deflowering the virgins and that he was only performing his duty as king. Mama Ocllo was in no way convinced, for had he not recently had the body of one of these women, who had died in childbirth, carried to a shrine on the road to the east? And had he not ordered young girls to be sacrificed there? The queen pictured the priest uncovering the breast of the little victim and plunging in his knife to cut out her heart. This blood homage to a rival was insupportable. 'But it is the law', the old ladies of her suite repeated. This was no consolation, for her own heart was not destined to besmear an idol's features with red blood. She loved and suffered for her love. Mama Ocllo prepared herself with very great care each time the king might come to see her. But would he come as usual for the evening meal and eat toasted maize and cakes?

A lady-in-waiting came to say that the all-powerful Inca was in conference with the high priest and the augurs in preparation for the feast of the Sun, the *Inti Raymi*, which was now near. The queen bowed, and to hide her vexation she asked that one of her favourite laments should be sung—perhaps the very one about the deceived lover which Huaman Poma records.

'Father Condor, take me,
Father Falcon, carry me away;
Tell my dear mother.
I have not eaten for five days,
Nor drunk a mouthful.
Father messenger, bearer of tokens, swift carrier,
Take away from me, I beseech thee, my mouth, my heart,
Take me, I beseech thee, to my father and mother'.

With fast-moving rhythm the melancholy voice continued the song. Through the door Mama Ocllo watch the dusk creep over the garden and envelop the golden statues with a trembling shadow which seemed to bring them to life.

Tupac Yupanqui was not any more devout than other people, but he paid honour to the shrines, worshipped Viracocha, and was willing to converse with the spirits after he had seen the Rimac idol. He had also made the pilgrimage to the islands[1] of Lake Titicaca, where there were statues of the Sun and Moon. But the two principal feasts of the year were for him, as for all the Inca kings, those of the winter and summer solstices. The Sun was the ancestor and founder of the dynasty, and so his changes of position directly interested his children, who were disturbed when he went away towards the north or south, and happy each time he returned. The regularity of the solstices and equinoxes should have calmed their anxieties, since the *quipou* experts had very probably adjusted the solar year (ideal) to the lunar year (practical), and they did not make mistakes in their calculations. But you never know with gods! Besides, the astronomers carefully watched the movements of the sun. With the aid of a stone column they measured the angle made by its shadow with a line drawn east and west. They also observed its rising and setting within the framework of sixteen towers erected each side of Cuzco, and this dial enabled them to follow the path of the luminary with great exactitude. Tupac Yupanqui visited his officers of the sky from time to time and discussed their work with them. He was not without humour. 'Why does the Sun', he asked, 'never weary of travelling about the sky, and why does he never change his route? He is like an animal on a lead who always follows

[1] The islands of Titicaca and Coati.

the same track'.[1] If a peasant had put this question he would have been burned alive, but coming from an Inca king, it was only a family joke.

However on the day when Mama Ocllo hid her impatience with her husband by listening to poetry, the king was in no mood for joking. The priests had decreed a fast. The sun, having reached the northern extremity of his course, was now returning to his people, and all must be made ready to celebrate this event. In a room in the palace where gilded walls reflected the flames of copal torches, Tupac Yupanqui received the officials who had come to make their reports. The llamas destined for the people were on the way, the maize liquor was fermenting, the virgins were preparing the biscuits and little loaves, and the headmen and the provincial controllers had been informed of the order of the ceremony.

'And the music?' asked the king.

The chief of the trumpeters said that his men were in good wind.

'Is all arranged for the dances?' demanded the sovereign.

A young man with gold circles in his ears was brought in to give an account of the provincial teams who had come with their *kenas,* flutes of reeds or baked clay with seven holes, their drums and their bells. There were, too, some peasants from the east who played Pan pipes[2] of all sizes, and they had brought with them gourds full of grain. Satisfied with these preparations and confident that all was ready for the next day, Tupac Yupanqui rose, and with a glance at the backs of the bowing officials, went to his private apartments. No *Coya* and no concubine this night, for chastity must be observed on the eve of *Inti Raymi.*

On the central square all the Inca's family, the royal *aylu,* was crouching with arms crossed and with palms turned towards the east. Tupac Yupanqui alone was standing upright, intoning a prayer, which the faithful took up in chorus. The first ray of the sun had just touched the roofs of Cuzco. A murmur went up from the neighbouring streets, and the people took up the words of thanksgiving. Little by little, as the light spread over the town, so did the voices of a hundred thousand Indians. Then a great cry went up, '*Hailli!* Victory'. All the people of Cuzco down to the humblest citizen knew that at that moment the king was raising a

---

[1] Quoted by Garcilaso, according to Blas Valera.

[2] The Pan flute, with five to twelve pipes, or sometimes with a series of pipes banded together. The syrinx (Antara in Quechua) was made of reeds, baked clay, or even stone. The Incas endeavoured to establish the pentatonic scale.

Fig. 43. The Inca king offers the sacred drink to the Sun

golden cup towards the Sun. What would they not have given to see Tupac Yupanqui make this unique gesture of offering or consecration!

The gold cup contained the maize drink, the wine of the Incas, blessed by the Sun. The king poured this into a jar, also of gold, and then with his left hand he filled a cup and drank. His family then stood up and, one by one, tendered a goblet of precious metal to the sovereign. The king filled it, after letting the liquid pour over his right hand—the hand of the Sun. The man or woman drank a mouthful and then knelt prostrate. After the members of the royal house, the officials and headmen approached to receive the sacred drink and the king served them. Then a procession was formed which set out, with bare feet, to Curiancha, the temple of the Sun.

Only the size denoted the purpose of this building; it was constructed of grey stones, polished and arranged with care, and it isolated the world of the god and his priests. It was not a cathedral to which the people were admitted, but a family sanctuary, and even a family vault, for the mummies of the Peruvian kings were placed there for a relative eternity, seated on golden stools. The whole interior, which was kept hidden from the common people, was of gold: the tiles covering the walls, the framework of the roof, the effigies of the gods, and the ornaments of the high priest, *Villac huma*. At this moment he was standing in front of the single door of the temple, surrounded by those who made the sacrifices and by soothsayers. When the procession appeared at the other side of the square he bowed his head and awaited the king. Tupac Yupanqui handed to him his golden cup, and the members of the royal family gave their goblets to the priests, who collected them, or rather took possession of them, for these objects were offerings to the servants of the god. The king looked at the high priest attentively. This old man, stooping under the weight of a golden crown, a cloak and a white robe encrusted with precious stones, his arms bearing bracelets, and the lobes of his ears drawn downwards by rings of gold, this symbolic and gorgeous object was the king's uncle, the brother of the late Inca Pachacutec. Some years before, he had angered the king by his continual interference in the affairs of state, so the king decided to restrain his functions and limit them to the cult of the Sun. Besides, on the day of the *Inti*, it was he, the king, who became the pontifical ruler, and the priest was his subordinate.

Tupac Yupanqui entered the temple, whilst the headmen placed their offerings at the door: statuettes of sheep, birds, toads or snakes, all, of course, fashioned in gold or silver. The king advanced to the altar which had been erected facing the east. The image of Viracocha stood above it, framed by a sun with a human face and an oval moon. Other motifs represented the morning star, the Pleiades, and a lake, no doubt Titicaca, the cradle of the dynasty. The moment had come to beseech the ancestor for some token of his presence. A petty monk the *valla visa,* placed a bundle of kapok on the altar, and the high priest held a concave mirror above it. The rays of the sun concentrated on the white fibres and caused them to burst into flames. At once the news, which was communicated to the crowd by the priests, spread throughout Cuzco, and Tupac Yupanqui heard as a murmur of joy, the *haillis* which broke out around the temple. Sceptics will say that if it had rained, how would the fire have been made? In June it does not rain. If unfortunately the sky was cloudy, the *valla visa* used the necessary means to make a fire, for one must lend the gods a hand at times. But on this particular day the ceremonies went off without any hitch, and everything pointed to the oracles being favourable. This was the essential point of the religion.

Four officiating priests led a black llama to the altar and presented it to the king, who made a gesture of acceptance, and the *tarpuntay* who had been selected to slaughter the animal performed his office. The llama shook convulsively between the eight arms which upheld it, but the priest quickly seized the lungs and flung them on the altar. The soothsayer, *Calparicoc,* came from his cell with the decoction of bark or grain[1] which he used to put himself into a trance still frothing on his lips. He trembled and his words, uttered in a high voice, would not have been understood by anyone had not the *Villac huma* explained them. The king listened patiently to these diplomatic oracles; he knew that an easy war and a favourable peace would be foretold.

'This year the blind will only see a little, the deaf will hear fairly well, and the rich will be a little better than the poor'.

These pontifical utterances are those of Alcofribas, it is true, but were the high priest's words any more explicit? If the drops of blood on the stones had a favourable meaning, yes, but if unfavourable, no. The *Inti Raymi* was the feast of hope and nothing would

[1] A datura or the seeds of *Piptadenia colubrina.*

alter the king's optimism. The *Villac huma* and the other priests of the Sun were too wily to break this happy tradition.

The trumpets sounded outside the temple to signify to the people that the religious ceremonies were over. Immediately the llamas from the royal herd were killed and distributed to the visitors, with maize bread and fermented drink. The feast began. It was the hour, provided for by law, when everyone could, indeed must, laugh, sing, drink, dance and be happy. And happiness lighted up the austere faces of the officials, of the soldiers on leave, of the marriage-able girls, and even the prostitutes who had slipped out of their reserved quarter. Amongst the crowd, people from the provinces wandered about, holding on to each other's tunics so as not to get lost. One saw people from the south with their little pointed caps, the inhabitants of Pissac clad in little red and black capes and wearing wide hats, delegations from the tropical lands with their faces painted white or hidden behind animal masks. Some of them, whose tribe had surrendered only recently, stood timidly round their headmen. But the *chicha* which was distributed at street corners and at the gates of palaces soon loosened tongues and the groups chatted with one another. Drums sounded and the lilting of flutes broke forth like a flight of humming birds.

All Cuzco began to dance, the people from the provinces in their own groups, taking no notice of their neighbours. The citizens danced as they pleased to the fast rhythm of the *yass*. The women, stamping the earth, revolved gracefully in front of their husbands, and soon the men joined them, only stopping to swallow a bumper of fermented drink. The young girls ventured in their turn, and they were met with smiles and compliments or invitations to make love.

'I will put your feet into a woollen sandal!' This was the gesture of a young man on his wedding night when he married a virgin. A joker cried, 'Put her rather in a boot of *ichi!*' This field herb was used as a nuptial shoe for women who were not virgins, and the people shouted with laughter. Whilst the music went on an argu-ment broke out between two young people. 'Llamas hooves!' cried the first. '*Iqu,* unwelcome!' replied the other. The bystanders took sides and insults took the place of jests. Each district had its own special expression. 'Toad's stomach'. 'Invert'. This last sally, a pecu-liarly unpleasant one, brought an immediate reply. 'How are the children I gave your wife?' At this point verbal assault gave way to brawling—primitive and brutal fisticuffs which did not stop the dancing. But there was a risk that the two groups of opponents would go off to a field in the suburbs and finish out the quarrel with slings.

For two days and nights the capital rejoiced. This was just long enough to bring the people to the saturation point of dancing, drinking, and liberty. The automatism of work succeeded to the automatism of pleasure. And when, at dawn on the third day, the sun shone on the daily llama sacrifice, the citizens took the road to their labours. Only the villagers from the east danced on, entranced by the sober melodies of their pipes, prisoners to the obsessive cadence of their round. The Inca's personal guards shepherded them gently towards the path which would lead them home.

In the damp rooms where they knotted the cords of their *quipous* the agricultural officials of the southern zone listened to the music dying away in the distance. Suddenly there was only silence around them and the voice of their leader repeating monotonously, so very monotonously, 'Two loads of potatoes have arrived from the village of Checca. Half is for the smelters' warehouse'. Cuzco went on with its work.

CHAPTER XII

A GOD DESERTS HIS PEOPLE

*The heir to the throne goes out hunting–He joins his father in the
north of the Empire–The king explains the rights and duties of conquest–A relief map–Huayna Capac's family life–The golden chain of
the Incas–The king divides his realm–Doubt and scepticism*

□

W H I L S T the king was campaigning in the northern part of the
Empire, the prince, his son and heir, was hunting llamas near Cuzco.
His was a rich personality ! His name denotes this—Huayna Capac
—'A young man endowed with great gifts'. There was nothing surprising in the fact that he began his royal career by hunting game.
Two or three thousand Indians armed with sticks drove the herds
of vicuñas towards the hill where the hunters were stationed. As
soon as the circle of beaters was closed, the prince and his friends
took their nets and aimed at the strongest beasts. Their capture was
not easy, for llamas have a strong kick, and when they are enraged
spit out a sticky saliva. Huayna Capac liked nothing better than to
overcome the big males and throw them to the ground. Of course he
always had a faithful servant beside him ready to kill any refract-
ory game with his spear. About twenty captured beasts was the
usual bag in this princely sport. The hundreds of others which were
captured were handed over to the shearers and a small number to
the butchers[1]

When he returned from these open-air expeditions, which were
all too few for his liking, the prince rejoined his young wife, and
aided by sweet music, they endeavoured to provide a grandson for
the king. Indeed, Yupanqui had expressed his desire to be a grandfather and was impatient because so far he had not been obeyed.
But neither the palace doctors nor the singers of nostalgic *yaravis*
had been able to overcome the princess's sterility. So Huayna
Capac was not surprised when the chief of the messengers knelt
before him, a red thread in his hand and a message from the king

[1] Certain hunts were held annually ; thirty thousand Indians, or sometimes
more, took part. The wool from the shorn vicuñas was placed in the king's
stores.

on his lips. He ordered his son to join him at Tumebamba, a town in the province of the Canaris, 400 leagues north of the capital, with an army of 12,000 men. The moment had come to think of serious affairs—war.

The gentle princess wept and begged the ladies of her suite to do likewise when her twenty-year-old husband left the capital. Huayna Capac had the choice of two routes to the north, and he decided to take the central road across the high plateaux, for this was in perfect condition for over 1,000 miles, while several granaries belonging to the commissariat would ensure his supplies. His advance was swift, for in the plains and on the plateaux the way was so well paved that the bearers scarcely rocked the litters of their captains. The bridges of aloe fibre had been doubled and the troops lost no time in crossing river torrents. North of Jauja, however, an annoying bottle-neck occurred. The only means of passing from one bank to the other was by a system of baskets suspended from a cable. Each basket held only four men, and in spite of the efforts of expert officers who operated the ropes, several days of coming and going were necessary before they could re-form the army. When they reached the country of the Huamachucos, the road, which had been broad enough to permit seven or eight men to march abreast, now narrowed, and its irregular paving tired the porters. Frequently, in order to cross a pass the road became a staircase. Huayna Capac now realised how swift had been the great Pachacutec's conquest of these regions. But on the plain of Cajamarca the troops found the paving stones well set on an embankment with low walls on either side. At last, two months after his departure from Cuzco, the prince saw before him the palace of Tumebamba, where his father awaited him.

Tupac Yupanqui rejoiced to see his son, for of his five legitimate sons and his 200 children by his concubines, Huayna Capac was the favourite, and although he was not the eldest, the king had designated him as heir to the throne. He declared his satisfaction with the long march the prince had accomplished at the head of 12,000 men. Then gathering around him some of his wise men and his suite, he publicly made an important statement to his son.

'Your ancestor Roca, who, as you know, was stout, a lover of good living and of women, had a very lively intelligence. He was the first of our dynasty to bear the title *Sapa*, the great man. I will remind you of one of his sayings, of which, by reason of my age, I have understood the real meaning. "Ambition does not enrich, but impoverishes the mind, for it deprives it of the advice of honest people". Look around you and you will see our faithful servants. They will explain to you our recent campaigns. But since you are about to take a part in war, and the responsibility for the armies will henceforth fall on you, you must learn from my own lips the difficulties we have encountered. Tomorrow you will be faced with them yourself. Listen well. Here we are at the gates of a new country whose inhabitants are fine warriors. You see this metal axe; if I had been less skilful in combating the soldiers who handle this weapon, we should be mourning many more deaths amongst our men. But these men of the Canaris tribe—for that is their name— also know how to melt gold and work it with skill. They make vessels and gold plates ornamented with the Chavin god, and also teeth which they set in the jaws of their dead. They have other customs which will surprise you, amongst them that of sacrificing hundreds of children in front of the cave where, they say, their god has a permanent dwelling. This tradition should be respected so long as it does not eliminate too many workers for the Incas. But you will soon learn to decide what must be kept and what must be suppressed amongst the customs of the tribes you may conquer. Thus, at the time of my two first campaigns towards the south, one towards the river Paraguay, the other towards the deserts which reach to the sea,[1] I did not hesitate to impose the whole of our laws where I was able to do so, for you must understand that the coastal inhabitants were rather a trial to us. Amongst the Huamachucos, who live to the east of the road you travelled, there was no reason why their beliefs should not be completely changed, for apart from the snakes they worshipped and the stags' horns they cut off as hair ornaments, they were of no special interest. As for the Chachapoyas . . .'

The king stopped speaking and shut his eyes. As the water of a lake ripples in the wind, his face trembled with a sudden emotion. Huayna Capac looked at his father and found him very weary and very old.

The king continued, 'We crossed a broad torrent at the bottom of a valley.[2] It was so hot that the soldiers took off their tunics and

[1] As far as Chile.
[2] The Marañon, the upper stream of the Amazon, as far as the present village of Balsas.

began to scale the wooded bank opposite. But two days later, the vanguard, camping at the top of a pass, had to endure a snow blizzard and 300 men were buried and died. The gods of the Chachapoyas are powerful, my son! And they were hostile to us throughout the expedition. At times it seemed that Viracocha and our father the Sun had abandoned us to our enemies. I assaulted many fortresses, but at each attempt men with fair skins stoned us from their ramparts, or threw themselves upon our soldiers with such frenzy that we had to break off the combat and take refuge near the river. They never exploited their success, for they were not used to fighting or living anywhere but on the heights. I admit that their dislike of descending to the valleys spared us a cruel defeat. It also allowed us to reach their capital but not to remain masters of it. You must return to that vast country'.

After a long silence, which Huayna Capac did not dare to break by asking questions, the king continued: 'This is necessary for three reasons. First the country is rich: sweet fruits, coca, maize and potatoes grow from the bottom to the top of the same mountain slope. Secondly the inhabitants are worthy to belong to the Empire; the men work stone as well as the people of Cuzco, and are knowledgeable about gold. The women are beautiful, and their customs admirable. I shall never forget the villages with their round houses built in tiers, their fortresses well situated against the rock and sometimes commanded by a tower. And above all the monuments, which are built on the high cliffs and which appear inaccessible. When you see them you will be reminded of our *huacas*. These are tombs where they enclose the mummified bodies of their chiefs and priests.[1] The dead have no other company but the wind and the condor—for the condor is their god. The third reason which compels you to undertake the campaign is that you are my son. In a short time you will be crowned with the royal turban, and your duty will be to subdue those who have rejected the laws of the Incas'.

'I will do this!' cried the prince. 'I will wipe them out!'

'No,' said the king, 'you must not exterminate those who can render service; you must conquer them. War is necessary to occupy our subjects and to allow us to acquire new wealth. But war is above all a means of spreading the benefits of our laws. It is our absolute duty to make them known in all countries. Do not forget

---

[1] Anthropomorphic funerary monuments, numerous in the region of Chachapoyas and the river Utcubamba.

that behind our armies come the controllers, the professors, the judges and priests. Officials, my son, who will more completely subdue the Chachapoyas and the rest than your soldiers. Today our adversaries are no longer herdsmen or wanderers such as our ancestor Manco Capac saved from ignorance. It may perchance happen that we shall meet cannibals on the outskirts of the virgin forest, but this is a very rare occurrence—although men devouring one another is rather an amusing sight. The people whom you will bring to submission are in many respects our equals in the art of weaving and working gold. Do not worry about this, for these things are proof of their patience and of the wealth lying in their soil. The enemy is not to be feared for his virtues but for his pride, and strange as it may seem, many Indians are persuaded that their way of life is the best in the world; it is up to us to alter this belief. It is certain that our slings, spears, and above all our helmets will aid the newcomers to accept the advantages of the Inca law. But believe me, that is not enough, and I will give you an example'.

At the king's orders, four servants brought an enormous map, made in relief from modelled clay. The northern part of the Empire, with its plains and ranges of mountains, was represented on it. Huayna Capac touched a stone set in the clay and asked, 'We are here?'

'Yes', replied the king, 'you will see that the clay round your finger is still fresh, for each day our envoys bring in new information which enables us to correct the course of a river or smooth out the shape of a mountain. I want to talk to you about the country of the Chimus. In preparation for my expedition, I took care to subdue all the mountainous country which bounds it on the east. I used the old tactics of our ancestors, which was to obtain control of the Cordilleras before risking action on the sides. Then I sent envoys to the chief of the Chimus, asking him not to oppose the advance of my troops. He knew with what gentleness your grandfather, Pachacutec, treated the people of Rimac, and even those of Huara. He knew also that my army was double the size of his. But he refused to surrender, even for such good reasons, claiming that his god, Kon, was greater than Viracocha, and said that he would cause us to withdraw to the mountains. I was obliged to give battle. Our losses were cruel, chiefly because the battles had to be fought in a very hot climate, which upset our soldiers. Do you know how I came to make terms with the enemy? I held separate parleys with each of the Chimu generals. I showed them that their resistance was useless and above all I promised them important posts in the Inca administration if they would compel their king to lay down his arms. They were very flattered, and they were also as proud of themselves as a parrot is of his feathers. They were able to convince their king, who came and knelt before me and agreed to accept the Sun as his god. Of course I had the generals executed for betraying their people, and I allowed the ruler to keep some of his rights. You have learned of these things at the *Yacha huasi,* but you do not know of the trouble the Chimus caused us once their territory was occupied. These sheep were transformed into tigers! All they would talk about to our officials was the deeds of their god, the conquests of their ancestors, and the trade they once carried on with the people of Tiahuanaco, and even with the northern part of the country. They boasted of the skill of their sailors, whom, to hear them talk, you would have thought had sailed their rafts to distant islands. They were proud of their brick houses, their towns with their gardens, and the artificially made hills where their princes resided. In spite of our threats, they went often to their temples, and hid their idols, so as to worship them on the shore at night. Even when reduced to poverty, they found ways of caring for their clothes, decking themselves with jewels, with rings in their noses and shoulder straps of gold. To defy us, the peasants went into the fields wearing soldiers' helmets, which covered their temples with great metal discs. Merchants continued to sell plants and ornaments, accepting shells as payment and so escaping the control of our officials. This went on in all parts of their vast country, at Parmunca, the frontier city in the south, as well as at Chanchan their capital, and also at Moche where the oldest Chimu tribes lived, and who were worshippers of the Sun and Moon. Even in the far north where the provinces bore different names, and whose people, before our arrival, had hated the Chimus, even there the inhabitants put up a resistance to our officials which could not be broken. The occupation of their country had given the Chimus back a pride in their past, and against this feeling, my son, there is no weapon but time'.

As the king stopped speaking, Huayna Capac looked at the men around them. Their faces remained impassive. Each of them was one of his father's advisers; they were responsible for tactics, strategy, armament, roads, agriculture, astronomy, history, and

Fig. 44. The Inca Empire at its zenith

justice. Almost all of them bore in their ears the golden rings of the royal family. They directed the greatest Empire in the world. The prince gently touched the relief map with his hand. He thought of the long road he had covered at the head of his troops, and he seemed to hear the noise of the wind on the high plateaux, the rustling of water or of leaves in the depths of the valleys, the songs of his soldiers. His journey had been a young man's lighthearted undertaking, a care-free adventure. Only today did he understand the meaning of conquest, and the heavy burden he must now assume. He knelt before the king, as did the most respectful of his subjects, and asked leave to kiss his feet.

This gesture of humility Huayna Capac directed towards his sovereign, not his father. As soon as he was himself invested with his royal dignities, he exacted a similar reverence from everyone. He had such a high conception of his office as the Great Inca that he had two of his brothers killed because they were accused of refusing to attend the coronation ceremony. The gentle Rava Ocllo, for whom his youthful heart had beat so strongly, but who seemed to be definitely sterile, had also to suffer for reasons of state. Huayna Capac chose one of his nieces as his second legitimate wife, Mama Runtu. There were some murmurs from amongst the members of the royal family, but the wise men upheld the king. This decision had happy consequences, for Rava Ocllo, with that flair for the appropriate which serves jealous women for logic, gave birth to a fine son before her rival had time to get to work. Huayna Capac, indifferent to the subtlety of the feminine heart, rejoiced loudly.

In his joy, he showed mercy to the people of Tumbes and Huancavilica, in the north of the Chimu country, who had risen against their judges and controllers. Had the law been strictly applied they would have been burned or stoned, but Huayna Capac contented himself with having four teeth extracted from the chiefs responsible for the revolt, 'two from the top and two from the bottom'. Thus they were the living witnesses of their own perfidy and the king's generosity. It was an act of great wisdom which the people of the province welcomed with acclaim—they even sought to imitate their chiefs, and all the people of Huancavilica had four teeth extracted. The whole Empire benefited from the paternal kindness of the Inca, and for a month the distribution of meat and maize alternated with celebrations. Even at Cuzco the officials smilingly marvelled at the new order of things; if they did not go so far as to be openly gay, it was because they knew how changeable a prince's moods could be.

But Huayna Capac wanted to celebrate in striking fashion the ceremony of the first cutting of the hair which accompanied the weaning of children. On this occasion it was traditional in the royal family to gather together in the central square at Cuzco and sing the praises of the sovereign. Two or three hundred men, all with the golden rings in their ears, took each other by the hand and danced before the king in dignified fashion. The music was only a prolonged chanting which recalled the good deeds of the reigning Inca and his ancestors. Huayna Capac had the idea of completing the circle of his family by a gesture at once allegorical and magnificent; they would hold a golden chain as they danced. He summoned the chief of the goldsmiths and gave him two years to melt and cut a 'golden chain 700 feet long, each link of which would be the size of a man's fist'. The good general Cusi Hualpa, whose recollections are the origin of this story, asserted that he saw it in the hands of the Inca nobility as they sang in harmony the praises of their master and sought the blessing of Viracocha[1] on the head of the royal infant. But that day the god of the Incas must have been directing his attention to other things. Perhaps he was watching the disembarkation of Yanez Pinzon on the coast of Brazil on the other side of the continent. Or perhaps he was present in an even more distant land at the birth of a future emperor of Peru, Charles the Fifth. The world beyond the frontiers of his own people was disturbed. In the square at Cuzco, the Inca raised his son above the kneeling crowd and gave him the name of Huascar. But it is known that the golden chain, symbol of the king's greatness and of the obedience of his subjects, was not a happy omen for the prince. The time was not far off when he would be burdened with less glorious fetters.

Did Huayna Capac have some inkling of the drama which was being prepared in the mysterious future? Was he advancing towards the hour of disaster as blindly as the foreign invaders towards the hour of triumph? No doubt the soothsayers had warned him of a danger which earthquakes and the appearance of comets foretold

---

[1] The gold chain disappeared. It is not known if the conquerors melted it with the rest of their booty, or whether the Indians hid it in a cave or at the bottom of a lake in the Cordilleras.

as being at hand. But the king was convinced of his own glory, and more than any other Inca he had in front of him the spectacle of men kneeling before him or bent over their work. The Aymara miners, the Nasca potters, the Cuzco goldsmiths, the builders of fortresses and of roads, peasants and poets, all carried out their duties to perfection, and precautionary measures and controls worked smoothly. The Empire had never been so big nor so perfectly organised. But Huayna Capac had not the firm assurance of his ancestors. At times he hesitated between two decisions, as if one or the other might lead him into a fatal mishap. A woman's influence, as was the case with the rebellious Chachapoyas, made him indulgent to his enemies. But at times he was ruthless in subduing a rebellion; he had the inhabitants of the island of Puna, opposite Tumbes, impaled and cut in pieces, and he had 2,000 Caranquis drowned in a lake. These Indians, who lived in the extreme north of the Empire, had an inexplicable vice—idleness—although their morals were no lower than those of the Esmeraldas, river-dwellers from the coast, who practised sodomy and married only girls who had co-habited with their fathers. But the king paid these people the compliment of sending them teachers. The reign of Huayna Capac is full of such contradictions.

His own family life did not exhibit the traditional Inca customs. Already possessed of two legitimate wives and an abundant reserve of concubines, he fell in love with a maiden of the Caras tribe who had pleased him one evening, and he installed her in his palace at Quito. This capital of the northern province became the residence of the royal pair and a son was born to them there—Atahualpa. This boy would have become one of the nobly born bastards who filled high official posts, but paternal affection made him a prince and even co-heir.

The *amautas* who were established at Cuzco and who discussed the ruler's actions could not understand this aberration. Could not the king realise that for the first time since its foundation the unity of the Empire was threatened? Or did Huayna Capac seek to establish an independent state? They came to Quito to express their fears, but they found a hostile court and other wise men whose wisdom seemed to them folly. What was to be done? The king was far too occupied with his fight against the Caranquis, who had recently rebelled, and against a number of the Cara tribes, who were oblivious of the fact that one of their young girls had married the Inca. The Caras were ruthless enemies and were supported by the Chibchas,[1] a neighbouring powerful and highly developed race.

The ambassadors from Cuzco returned there very disturbed by what they had seen. For the way was long—very long—and how fragile in its immensity seemed the Tawantinsuyu, the Four Quarters of the World! Where the Inca lived there was the Empire. What would happen if Huayna Capac abandoned his legitimate capital in the same way as he had abandoned his two legitimate wives and the heir to the throne? All their hopes were centred on the young Huascar, the studious pupil of the *Yacha huasi*. Huascar!

Yielding to the urgings of his grand council, the king left Quito for a time and came to Cuzco to celebrate the feast of the Sun. He was received with the customary enthusiasm, and the *Inti Raymi* ceremony began. But as the sun ascended from the horizon and the crowd sang the hymn of thanksgiving, Huayna Capac remained motionless, his eyes fixed on the blinding luminary. The high priest beside him said, 'Inca, what are you doing? You must not gaze at our father in that way'. But the king did not move. 'Take care!' cried the priest. Huayna Capac lowered his eyes to the *Villac huma* and smiled, and later, after the sacrifices, he summoned him to the palace.

'I have two questions and two questions only to put to you', he said. 'First, would one of my subjects dare to order me to leave my throne each morning and make me run throughout the day?'

'Such a man would be mad', replied the high priest.

'And if', continued the king, 'I ordered the most powerful of my nobles to march into Chile, would he not obey?'

'He would obey you to the death', replied the high priest.

'Very well', cried the Inca, 'our father the Sun runs across the sky each day without stopping. If he were ruler of all the things in our world, he would stop when he wished and rest. Since he does not, he must depend on a more powerful god than himself. Ought we to entrust our life and the life of the country to the Sun?'

The high priest was silent. He appeared crushed by this incomprehensible sacrilege. But as the king was dismissing him with a gesture, he said in a trembling voice, 'Your father, Tupac Yupan-

---

[1] The Chibchas, masters of a great part of present-day Colombia, were conquered by the Spaniards (the Quesada expedition) in 1536.

qui, evidently thought like you, but he never gave utterance to such terrible words'.

A few days later Huayna Capac set off for Quito. He embraced his son Huascar and thought him a fine young man, but twenty days later he would hold his other son, Atahualpa, in his arms. He too was a son to be proud of!

That year a warm breeze spread seeds of doubt, of forgiveness, and of scepticism across the world. On the banks of European rivers, pleasure palaces replaced fortresses; Leonardo da Vinci devised locks and canals; La Giaconda began a long and smiling career; Machiavelli published *The Prince*.

The Peruvian Indians breathed this same air, which gave a new meaning to life and death. Perhaps Huayna Capac or one of his sons would become the prince of an Indian Renaissance.

But that year a band of wandering knights, their armour drenched with Pacific spray, gazed towards the southern lands. Amongst them there was a captain called Francisco Pizarro.

CHAPTER XIII

THE INCA STORY CONTINUES

The search for and discovery of Machu Picchu–Peruvian soil contains wonderful secrets–Visit to the men of the clouds–The little boy in the country of Huaman Poma

☐

THE morning of July 24, 1911, was cold. The mist covered the bottom of a valley where the rapid current of the river Urubamba foamed over the stones. A young American, Hiram Bingham, and a Peruvian policeman, Sergeant Carrasco, were gazing at the slope of a mountain they were about to climb. The ascent was steep, the path narrow, but their guide was certain that they would find ruins at the top. Twenty times before Bingham had undertaken similar explorations, from which he had returned thrilled but unsatisfied. What he was looking for was not a simple fortress or a temple but a capital city—an Inca city.

Study of the writings of our old companion of past centuries, Father de la Calancha, had brought Bingham first to Cuzco and then to the Cordillera of Vilcapampa, which dominates the ancient capital of Peru to the north. He knew that an Inca prince had fled there after the Spanish conquest and had established a sort of headquarters of Indian resistance. This prince, the grandson of Huayna Capac, had received a hollow crown from Pizarro, but also a name which was famous—Manco. But in spite of his youth, Manco II had understood the part which the new masters of his country had reserved for him. He fled from Cuzco, accompanied by his nobles and an appreciable quantity of gold. After a few days, 10,000 Indians joined him in the Cordillera of Vilcapampa to which he had fled. A force was built up, ill clad, ill fed, with few arms, but nevertheless formidable. The hatred of an invader is often a more useful support than a good supply service! From this jungle of icy mountains and tropical valleys, little groups fell like devils on the Spanish convoys, breaking their horses' legs and killing the riders. Soon Manco felt himself strong enough to attack Cuzco, and his soldiers burned part of it by throwing white-hot projectiles from their slings. But the Spaniards counter-attacked and recaptured the fortress of Sacsahuaman, and the prince withdrew into the mountain. Legend says that he built a town far from the usual routes, so as to preserve the traditions of his ancestors.

What peak sheltered this mysterious city of the faithful? The two rivers flowing parallel to each other to the north and south of Cuzco, the Urubamba and the Apurimac, both enclosed the mountain range where Manco II had fled. On the side nearest to the Apurimac, the historical river of the Inca Empire, the French explorer, Eugène de Sartigues, and two Peruvian companions thought in 1814 that they had found the city in the ruins of Choquequirau. The place was wild and impressive, overshadowed by the snows of the Cordilleras. But there were no proofs that these huge houses and fortresses had sheltered the forces of the rebellious prince. The buildings dated from the Chanca war and had been fairly acquired by king Viracocha. On the slopes above the Urubamba, the researches were even more of a problem. The name Vitcos, given by certain chroniclers to Manco's city, had disappeared from maps from the 17th century onwards, and no one could be sure that it had ever existed other than in the imagination of the geographers. It was by chance that during one of the long journeys which he so much enjoyed, Charles Wiener was told of the existence of ruins near a mountain named Machu Picchu. He recorded this in his notebook and went on his way. Wiener was one of those who believed in the wonders of travel but not in making discoveries. Thirty years later, young Bingham had, on the contrary, a precise passion to satisfy, which was to find Manco's capital. Dr. Carlos Romero, a Lima historian, set him on the road by showing him, with wise and kindly intent, the writings of Father de la Calancha.

The American explorer was now on the point of making his discovery. His companions on the expedition, rather sceptical, did not trouble to accompany him—one was chasing butterflies and the other washing his shirts in the waters of the Urubamba. They thus deprived themselves of the pleasure of discovering one of the greatest monuments to human audacity and pride. Eighteen feet above the river, Bingham stumbled on the ruins of a house. Through the brambles and bushes shone light granite blocks of hewn stone. Nothing is more strange than to find stones bearing the marks of men of former times, already returning to the earth from which they were excavated. The American explorer thought that Machu

Picchu was a town which had half disappeared under vegetation
and mud. But when he climbed up to a terrace, he saw buildings
which had escaped the powerful upheaval of roots and the strangle-
hold of creepers. These buildings reminded him of the temple of
the Sun at Cuzco. Other monuments were built with blocks that
were huge at the base but were less so towards the top so as to
present a perfect impression of harmony. 'What an incredible

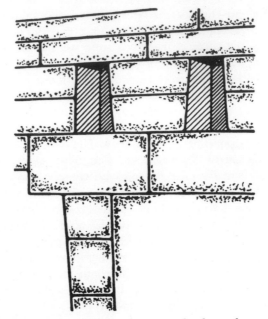

*Fig. 45. The blocks were huge at the base but smaller
towards the top*

dream!' cried Bingham. But every yard gained up the slope revealed
new wonders. When he reached a platform he saw two temples,
widely open on one side, while the three other sides had walls more
than twelve feet thick. There were trapezium-shaped (see figure
above) niches on the façade of one of the temples. The other temple
had three windows, very broad and accurately designed. The explorer remembered the phrase from a Peruvian writer of the 17th
century: 'Manco Capac, the first Inca king, gave orders for a wall
with three windows to be built at his birthplace'. In his excitement
at this discovery, Bingham awakened the spirits of the past. Spirits

are easy-going! But the Inca spirits already knew how to express themselves in the language of architecture, decorated pottery and metal tools. It was necessary only to study Machu Picchu to find there the elements of a sound theory of the origin of this redis-covered city.

This nest of stones clings to the eastern slope of a mountain crest at 8,000 feet. Two peaks protect its flanks, and at the bottom of the valley the river Urubamba surrounds it with a turbulent moat. The builders' desire for a defensive city is clear, but the period when they began to transport, shape, and adjust the rocks can only be guessed at. Pointed roofs, two storey-dwellings, and crudely erected walls suggest a pre-Inca origin. But, on the other hand, the general appearance of the buildings, the siting of the stones, the trapezium-shaped doors are in the most developed Cuzco style. The variety of the pottery is no help in solving the problem, for besides the big *chicha* jars and metal crucibles of Inca shape and ornamentation, dishes have been found of a foreign manufacture, especially Chimu, also designs coming from Amazonian sources. The virgin forest invaded the surrounding slopes, and butterflies and naked Indians became the neighbours of Machu Picchu.

The lay-out of the city does not satisfy our curiosity, but how imposing it is! The old houses of the town are grouped into rect-angular blocks which rise in terraces right to the top. Fifty stair-cases with 3,000 steps link the different quarters and lead to the temple with the three windows on the top-most platform of the *Intiwatana,* the 'stone which measures the sun'. The flights of steps are the streets of this city of the clouds. Alongside the evenly cut paving stone, water channels leap from step to step and hurl their waters down to the granite basins where the lizards now bask in the sun. For these streams have dried up and no traces of men or water have been left behind—or almost none. Fewer than 150 bodies have been found, 100 of them females, whom amateur historians have tried to identify as the chosen virgins who escaped from the *aclahuasi!* One day the excavators pick will open the huge mauso-leums and violate a silent collection of mummies. But today only tourists bring life to Machu Picchu. A railway carriage brings them from Cuzco to the foot of the mountain, and high above the ruins they find a little hotel where they can dream at nightfall of this mysterious countryside. Darkness transforms the town of the dead to the town of the sleeping. How much one would like to see the faces of the first inhabitants, listen to their voices, touch the muscles of the builders, join in their house-warming! Life alone mattered to them—this is what the monuments of Machu Picchu seem to say. Like the rest of the visitors we have to guess at their past. Before the Incas, this town existed as a modest and primitive village of a tribe which had broken away from the forest dwellers of the Amazon. Then other people occupied it, perhaps Chanchas who had escaped from pursuit by Viracocha after the bloody battle of Yahuarpampa. The whole range, overshadowed by the snowy summit of Salcantay[1] was the refuge of conquered and rebellious tribes. In pursuing them, the Incas certainly climbed the slopes of Machu Picchu, and on this predestined spot erected a fortress to control both the Cordilleras and the entrance to the virgin forest. Then according to a tradition of which Sacsahuaman is an example, they built a little town behind the ramparts. Generations of builders enlarged it, and astronomers, priests and virgins climbed there. It is not impossible that Manco II, the last rebellious Indian chief, took refuge there with his children, and they ended their life as hunted men in this high prison where they had the illusion of freedom.

But this only conjecture.

The discovery of Machu Picchu does not bring research into Inca civilisation to an end—far from it! In Peru and in the countries which were once in subjection to the kings of Cuzco, much evidence of the past has not yet yielded its secrets. Besides, all the manuscripts of the chroniclers and of the Spanish officials have not yet been read. The hour of the archeologist has hardly begun in South America, and it is certain that from now to the end of the century our knowledge will be enriched by discoveries and new interpretations. The Incas will be confirmed in their reputation as conquerors, organisers, great political administrators, but also as the legitimate inheritors of an Indian code of ethics unchanged through the centuries. We know already that the ways of life which preceded the Inca Empire, and of which two attempts at classification will be made later,[2] are illustrated by an infinite variety of details. Each of them corresponds to a sort of perfection of a technique or an art: pottery for the Nascas and the Mochicas, weaving for the

---

[1] Climbed by Bernard Pierre's expedition in 1952.
[2] Cf. Appendix.

Chimus, metallurgy for the Aymaras, navigation for the people on the north coast—and here we reduce to an extreme simplicity the expressions of the Indian thought. As far as actual knowledge is concerned, it is not possible to measure these old civilisations except by their successes. But it is plain that they did not limit themselves to a skill which more or less conformed with the genius of their people. Perhaps in the future we shall obtain a precise idea of all the elements which made up these pre-Inca cultures. We already possess many admirable instances.

Fig. 46. Fishing scene. Pre-Inca drawing

The story of old Peru will be continued, thanks to the researches of library workers and scholars, who, following the examples of the travellers of past centuries, will be inspired with love for the Indian past. La Condamine, in 1736, sent by the Academy of Sciences of Paris to measure the size of a meridian arc at the Equator, was impressed by the grandeur of the ancient monuments. This physicist and mathematician ended up by coming down the Amazon on a raft, just like any ordinary explorer passionately interested in nature and in men. Alexander Humboldt, the naturalist, d'Orbigny the biologist, and Raimondi the geographer submitted to the same magic charm and endeavoured to reach the heart of the Indian mystery. Clement Markham did the same, thanks to the texts of the chroniclers, which he brought out of their oblivion before he published in London, in 1910, his *Incas of Peru*. One man preceded him by half a century—the great, and one is almost tempted to say the heroic, Prescott, who lost his sight over the manuscripts and had to invent a special means of writing his *History of the Conquest of Peru*. The ethnologist Raphaël Karsten, who went to observe the Indians of the equatorial forest, turned later to the study of the Inca religion. Nearer to our own time, a professor of political economy, Louis Baudin, when staying at Quito as a young man, felt the awakening of a flame of curiosity which led him to search all the Spanish texts in order to draw up a remarkable picture of Inca socialism. Thanks to him, the confused ideas of the community system of the Peruvians gave way to a clear insight into State Socialism, a 'rational creation' directing the social relations of the Indians, and in spite of its despotism, 'conceived not only in the best interests of the sovereign, but in those of the whole people'.

One is perhaps astonished that after so many studies and summaries the Inca Empire and earlier civilisations should still be subjects for research. Has not everything been said? Certainly much has been repeated. But Peruvian soil still contains many reasons for astonishing us. The greed of the Conquistadors did not destroy everything—the Indians preserved many treasures which they hid and which will one day be found. Earthquakes, which covered up so many records of the Andean past, will one day bring them to light again, six or seven centuries later. This happened at Cuzco in 1950, when Pachacutec's palace suddenly emerged from the ruins. But above all, modern archeology, of which Julian Tello is the forerunner in his own country, will continue to reveal details which, little by little, will reconstruct for us an exact picture of the civilisations of Peru. The work of Dr. Valcarcel on the fortress of Sacsahuaman, where he has found and uncovered the huge defensive towers of which Garcilaso spoke; the researches of our friend Reichlen which link up in the province of Cajamarca with a tradition which the Créqui-Montfort mission had found illustrated in Bolivia; the diggings of American scholars south of Cuzco and in the Viru valley on the north of the Peruvian coast; the vast works undertaken by Rebecca Carrion and the Peruvian searchers at Anvon near Lima; the studies of Professor Dumezil, of Dr. Alencastre and our friend Jehan Vellard—all these efforts, among many others, are examples of the activity which is going on in the huge workroom of history which is Peru.

Soon the prophetic names which the experts have given to ancient Peruvian cultures will be only the chapter headings of the great book of the Indians—episodes in the living Indian adventure.

In company with my friends of earlier expeditions, Jean de Guébriant and Fred Matter, the call of the Cordilleras came to me once more in 1941, some months after the journey which took us to the head waters of the Amazon.

On the cliffs above the left bank of the Utcubamba—the river of joy—we were seeking to reach the caves outside which statues were placed like big white birds with folded wings. The ascent was steep and soon a rock wall prevented our advance. We were at the foot of the monuments which had so astonished the Inca Tupac Yupanqui and his soldiers when they were waging war against the Chachapoyas. The explorers of the end of the 19th century—Vidal Senèze, Noetzli and the Englishman Bandelier—had seen them and General Langlois had photographed them. A professor of Peruvian history, D. Pedro Castillo, had reached similar ones some years before us. When we were able to hoist ourselves to the level of the grottos, a strange sight met our eyes—six statues, with their bases touching, rose up like a sugar loaf. But the arms outlined along the body and the head with an aquiline nose showed the desire to represent each statue as a man. Except for the head, made from a mass of earth, grass, and stones, the statue was hollow, and a mummy was found inside held in a net suspended in some way from four stakes. Evidently the Indians had carried the mummified body up the cliff and had finally built this tomb around it in human form. Then they had tried to make the niche inaccessible, and from that time, from their solitary height, these deified creatures protected the Indians in the valley.

Near the monuments, buildings of an identical material were found in the hollows of the mountain. On the walls we could make out drawings—hunting scenes, mythological persons, the sun. Their inspiration, just like the hammock holding up the mummy, the way of burying the dead which recalled urn burial, and the conical form of the ruins which we later visited, were very clear indications of the Amazonian origins of the Indians who had settled in this region. It was possible even to place their arrival at a fairly recent era and to make it agree with the last great migration of Arawak or Carib tribes. If one dared to risk a date, one would say that the last inhabitants of Chachapoyas, those who resisted the Inca armies, settled here about the 6th or 7th century of our era—at a time in Peruvian history when the Mochica and Nasca civilisation was spreading along the coast of the Pacific Ocean, and the Tiahuanaco culture across the high plateaux.

In the course of his wanderings in the Cordilleras, the traveller can find many reminders which link him closely with the work of the Incas and their predecessors. At first sight it is difficult to separate the one from the other. Fortresses and temples erected in commanding spots above valleys or on gentle slopes near rivers all have the same forbidding and symmetrical appearance. One must examine the cutting or the carving of the stones, the technique of the materials, or the ornamentations on pottery in order to decide to what period of Indian history they belong. But the eye quickly accustoms itself. You learn to recognise the people with square fingers from Tiahuanaco as easily as the hideous sharpened teeth of the Chavin races. You understand the mythical fantasies of the early Nascas, the melancholy of the Chimus, and the voluntary moderation of the Incas. If you can avoid the numerous tourist routes in Peru and set off as we have often done in company with the muleteers of the *herredure* roads, you will penetrate so intimately into the Indian world of former times that it will soon become familiar to you. And what discoveries may rejoice your heart!

In 1947 I followed the course of the upper Marañon. This country of high plateaux and deep ravines was that which Tupac Yupanqui had conquered for the Inca Empire. But the ruins showed only occasional signs of the victorious soldiers of Cuzco. We were in the Chavin region, on the actual route of the great migrations from the virgin forest. The so-called civilisation of the upper Marañon was revealed by one fortress after another, which enclosed the head waters of the Amazon. I could only picture in imagination the peasants herding their cattle or setting out with their long *taclia* on their shoulders to work in their fields at cloud level, and imagine also their dances and their prayers. The collections of stones would have been incomprehensible had it not been for the presence of a young companion.

He was a lad with a copper-coloured face, gay and bright. He led me to some ruins which I could understand only after I had climbed up to the fort which protected them. It was an imposing town where 10,000 Indians must have lived. In the clean paved

streets were headless monuments, though their shape remained
intact. The boy called the town Garo. I thought of the dead city
of Huanuco, capital of a people whom Tupac Yupanqui had been
proud to conquer. His real name has come down to us in the form
'Yaro-vilca'—the god of Yaro.

I was looking at an old Indian capital. But to my emotion was
added the pleasure of knowing that it was probably the birthplace
of Huaman Poma, the Indian historian and artist who has faith-
fully kept us company during this journey into the past. He was
born at a time when the Spanish gunners had not yet disturbed the
Inca order, at a time when the Indians, seeing the first rays of the
sun, rejoiced in their hearts that a new day had been given them.

The boy was happy—I don't know why. Perhaps because a
humming bird was seeking nectar in the corolla of the wild lilies.
But I had only to look at him amongst the stones of his ancestors
to understand that the Indian story would have no other end but
the end of man himself.

LIST OF THE INCA KINGS

☐

MANCO CAPAC	*End of 11th century*
SINCHI ROCA	*12th century*
LLOQUE YUPANQUI	*End of 12th century*
MAYTA CAPAC	*13th century*
CAPAC YUPANQUI	*13th century*
INCA ROCA	*Early 14th century*
YAHUAR HUACAC	*14th century*
VIRACOCHA INCA	*14th century*
PACHACUTEC	*15th century*
TUPAC YUPANQUI	*15th century*
HUAYNA CAPAC	*1485–1525*
HUASCAR	*1525–1530*

ATTEMPTS TO CLASSIFY CHRONOLOGICALLY THE ANCIENT CIVILISATIONS OF PERU

□

1. *According to Rebecca Carrion Cachot*

ARCHAIC ERA	4000 to 2000 B.C.	Chavin–Huaylas–Pukara
INTERMEDIATE ERA	2000 to 1000 B.C.	Tiahuanaco–Paracas–Kollawa
CLASSICAL ERA	1000 B.C. to A.D. 400	Chimu (1 and 2) Muchik–Nasca–Cuzco
INCA ERA	A.D. 1000 to 1532	The definite character of the Inca era appeared in the 10th century

2. *According to Henry Lehmann*

	THE ANDES	NORTH COAST	CENTRAL COAST	SOUTH COAST
3000 B.C.		San Pedro Chicama Huaca Prieta	Aspero	
800 B.C.	Chavin	Cupisnique	Ancon 1 White on Red	Cavernas (Paracas)
200	Chanapata Chiripa Recuay Tiahuanaco (early) Pukara	Salinar Gallinazo Mochica 1 Mochica 2	Lima (early)	Necropolis (Paracas 2) Nazca 1 Nazca 2
1000	Tiahuanaco (classical)	Tiahuanaco (coastal)		Pacheco
1200	Cajamarca (epigonal)	Chimu (epigonal)	Ancon 2 Chancay	Ica (intermediate)
1450	Inca	Chimu	Chancay	Ica (late)
1532		Inca	Inca	Inca

BIBLIOGRAPHY

(PART ONE)

LOUIS BAUDIN : *La Vie de François Pizarre*, Paris, 1930.

JOSÉ DURAND : *Garcilaso, el Inca platonico*. Las Moradas, Lima, 1949.

MIGUEL DE ESTETE : *Noticia del Peru*, Quito, 1916.

GARCILASO INCA DE LA VEGA : *Comentarios reales*, Lisbon, 1609.

FRANCISCO DE JEREZ : *La Conquista*. (Extract from *Los Cronistas de la conquista*, Paris, 1938.)

PEDRO PIZARRO : *Relacion del descubrimiento y conquista del Peru*. (Extract from *Los Cronistas de la conquista*, Paris, 1938.)

H. W. PRESCOTT : *History of the Conquest of Peru*.

PEDRO SANCHO DE LA HOZ : *Relacion para S. M. de lo sucedido en la conquista y pacificacion de la Nueva Castilla*. (Extract from *Los Cronistas de la conquista*, Paris, 1938.)

ZARATE : *Historia del descubrimiento y de la conquista de la provincia del Peru*, Antwerp 1555 and Madrid, 1853.

(PART TWO)

JOSE DE ACOSTA : *Historia natural y moral de las Indias*, London, 1880.

BALBOA : *History of Peru*. (Manuscript cited by Prescott.)

A. BANDELIER : *Los Indios y las ruinas aborigenes cerca de Chachapoyas*, Lima, 1921.

LOUIS BAUDIN : *L'Empire socialiste des Incas*. (Institut d'ethnologie, Paris, 1928.)

JUAN DE BETANZOS : *Suma y naracion de los Incas que los Indios llamaron Capaccuna*, Madrid, 1880.

H. BINGHAM : *Lost City of the Incas*, New York, 1948.

F. BOAS : *Primitive art*, Oslo, 1927.

REBECCA CARRION CACHOT : *La cultura Chavin*. (Revista del Museo nacional, Lima, 1948.)
— *Paracas*, Lima, 1949.

CIEZA DE LEON : *Cronica del Peru*, Séville, 1553, Antwerp, 1554 and Madrid, 1853, 1880.

BARNABE COBO : *Historia del nuevo mundo*, Madrid, 1890–1893.

LA CONDAMINE : *Mémoire sur quelques anciens monuments du Pérou*. (Académie royale des sciences et belles-lettres, Berlin, 1748.)

G. DE CRÉQUI-MONTFORT : *Fouilles de la mission scientifique française à Tiahuanaco.* (Congrès des Américanistes, Stuttgart, 1904.)

BERTRAND FLORNOY : *Cuzco, ou le socialisme chez les Inka,* La Nef, Paris, 1946.

Handbook of South American Indians.

M. FREZIER : *Relation d'un voyage à la mer du Sud,* Paris, 1716.

GAMBOA : *History of the Incas.* (English translation, London, 1907.)

GARCILASO INCA DE LA VEGA : *Comentarios reales,* Lisbon, 1609 and Madrid, 1723.

— *Paginas escogidas.* (Bibliothèque de culture péruvienne, Paris, 1938.)

F. GUAMAN POMA : *Nueva cronica y buen gobierno* (Preface by Richard Pietschmann), Institut d'ethnologie, Paris, 1936.

— *Los Cronistas del Convento.* (Bibliothèque de culture péruvienne, Paris, 1938.)

RAOUL D'HARCOURT : *L'Amérique avant Colomb,* Paris, 1925.

— *La Musique des Incas et ses survivances,* Paris, 1925.

— *Liens archéologiques intercontinentaux en Amérique.* (Journal des Américanistes, Paris, 1953.)

HUMBOLDT : *Vues des Cordillères et monuments des peuples indigènes de l'Amérique,* Paris, 1816.

RAFAEL KARSTEN : *La Civilisation de l'empire inca.* (French translation, Paris, 1952.)

BARTOLOME DE LAS CASAS : *De las antiguas gentes del Peru,* Madrid, 1892.

H. LEHMANN : *Les Civilisations précolombiennes,* Paris, 1953.

L. LOCKE : *The ancient Quipu,* New York, 1923.

CLEMENT MARKHAM : *The Incas of Peru,* London, 1910.

P. A. MEANS : *La Civilizacion precolombiana de los Andes,* Quito, 1919.

A. MEILLET AND M. COHEN : *Les Langues du monde,* Paris, 1924.

A. METRAUX : *Contribution à l'ethnographie et à la linguistique des Indiens Uro d'Ancoaqui.* (Journal des Américanistes, Paris, tome XXVII.)

E. MINNAERT : *La Symbolique des vases des Nazca.* (Bulletin des Américanistes de Belgique, Bruxelles, 1932.)

CRISTOBAL DE MOLINA : *Relacion de las fabulas y ritos de los Incas,* London, 1873.

MONTESINOS : *Memorias antiguas del Peru.* (Madrid, 1882.)

NORDENSKIÖLD : *The secret of the peruvian Quipu,* Göteborg, 1925.

— *Le Quipou péruvien de musée du Trocadéro,* Paris, 1931.

E. PALAVECINO : *Areas y capas culturales en el territorio argentino,* Buenos Ayres, 1948.

RAMON PARDAL : *Medicina aborigen americana,* Buenos Ayres.

Polo de Ondegardo : *Relacion del lineage de los Incas.* (Translated by Markham, London, 1873.)

Posnansky : *Eine prähistorische Metropole in Südamerika,* Berlin, 1914.

A. Raimondi : *El Peru,* Lima, 1874.

H. and P. Reichlen : *Recherches archéologiques dans les Andes de Cajamarca.* (Journal des Américanistes, Paris, tome XXXVIII.)

Paul Rivet : *Les Éléments constitutifs des civilisations du nordouest et de l'ouest sud-américain,* Göteborg, 1924.

Paul Rivet and Arsandaux : *La Métallurgie en Amérique précolombienne.* (Institut d'ethnologie, Paris, 1946.)

P. Rojas Ponce : *Aribalo inkaico,* Lima, 1948.

G. de la Rosa : *Les Caras de l'Equateur.* (Journal des Américanistes, Paris, 1908.)

Santa Cruz Pachacuti : *Relacion de Antiguedades del Peru.* (Manuscript cited by Tschudi, Lima, 1918.)

Juan de Sarmiento : *Relacion de la sucesion y gobierno de los Incas.* (Manuscript cited by Prescott.)

V. Senèze and J. Noetzli : *Voyages en Equateur et au Pérou,* Paris, 1885.

J. Tello : *Antiguo Peru,* Lima, 1929.

— *Origen y desarollo de las civilizaciones prehistoricas andinus,* Lima, 1942.

— *Wira Kocha inka.* (Revista de estudios anthropologicos, 1923.)

Francisco de Toledo : Questionnaire and notes. (Cited by Tschudi.)

J. J. Tschudi : *Contribuciones a la historia del Peru antiguo.* (Spanish translation, Lima, 1922.)

M. Uhle : *Los elementos constitutivos de las civilizaciones Sudamericanas,* A. U. C., Quito.

— *El Ayllu peruano,* Lima, 1911.

L. Valcarcel : *El Cuzco précolombiano,* Cuzco, 1924.

H. V. Vallois : *Les Races humaines,* Paris, 1948.

Velasco : *Histoire du royaume de Quito,* Paris. 1840.

Jehan Vellard : *Etudes sur le lac Titicaca et les Indiens Uru.* (Institut français d'études andines, Lima, 1950–1951.)

E. Wagner and O. Righetti : *Archéologie comparée,* Buenos Ayres, 1946.

L. Wiener : *Pérou et Bolivie,* Paris, 1880.

INDEX